JOY
·FOR THE·
JOURNEY

Endorsements

Need encouragement? Need a laugh? Need an interesting take on life's happenings? These vignettes are for you. Dell Hyssong presents brief illustrations from real life that will leave you wanting more. As you read, may you discover the secrets of living life with *Joy for the Journey*.

—**Shelia Heil**, The Gospel Greats Radio Program Manager

As a speaker, I know life on the road. The experiences the Hyssongs have had on their journey ring true and are very entertaining. I love being able to pick up a book and just read a few stories at a time. Dell's writing is inspiring and real. Reading this book has given me *Joy for the Journey*!

—**Georgia Shaffer**, Author of *Taking Out Your Emotional Trash*, PA, Licensed Psychologist, and Christian Life Coach

Dell Hyssong's *Joy for the Journey* offers rich, heartfelt, just plain good stories that instantly grip your heart and refuse to let go. These genuine stories are just that: genuine. They are unique to the American lifestyle and offer a true-to-life glimpse at faithfully walking daily with our Lord and the blessings thereof. I've had the pleasure of attending services where the Hyssongs were ministering, and I remember how they blessed me with their gospel music. Dell's stories are nostalgic, patriotic, and down-home American. They remind me of the time when traditional values were still valued. Moreover, Dell's stories inspire us to see those days still occur so we can find *Joy for the Journey*.

—**Travis W. Inman**, author of *When Love Called* and *Shadows*

Some people have a special gift of seeing God at work, real-time, moment by moment. Others glide through life rarely noticing the hand of God moving at all. What makes Dell Hyssong's book, Joy for the Journey, so special is his ability to see God in everything. Here you will find a collection of personal short stories that will train your eye to be more God-conscious and joy-filled, despite whatever negative circumstances you may be facing.

When the motorhome the Hyssongs travel in across the country to perform Christian concerts was vandalized, and all their valuables were taken, God turned this miserable situation into a blessing. When the engine fan blade punctured their radiator on the way to a concert, a service manager had the opportunity to listen to one of their CDs lying on the dashboard. Two years later, they would meet that service manager again and hear how his life had been changed. These are just two of the spine-tingling stories that are sure to leave you with Holy Spirit goosebumps.

Read Joy for the Journey when the second fruit of the Spirit (joy) is running on empty. Read this book to learn how to be patient and trust that God is moving, even when you can't see Him clearly. But most importantly, read Joy for the Journey to be mentored in how to see God moving in your own life.

—**R. James Shupp,** pastor of the Movement Church of San Antonio and author of *Who Killed Your Church?* and *One Blinding Vision*

This is a great book with fantastic stories. God is at work. Follow the Hyssongs as they weave stories of their adventures with God. Each page will leave you with *Joy for the Journey.*

—**Shawn Kuhn** of SuzyQ Marketing Services

Hungry for some inspiring, hope-filled, and true-life stories of God at work among us? Me too. *Joy for the Journey* touched just the right spot in my heart and I know it will also touch yours.

—**Lori Stanley Roeleveld**, author of
Running from a Crazy Man (and other adventures traveling with Jesus) and Red Pen Redemption

JOY ·FOR THE· JOURNEY

Real Stories, Real People, Real Joy!

Three hundred sixty-five days a year on the road.
Two hundred fifty plus concerts. Traveling by
motorbus with four adults and two children.
Come with us and see why we have *Joy for the Journey*.

Dell Hyssong

NEW YORK

Joy for the Journey

Real Stories, Real People, Real Joy!

Published in New York, New York, by Morgan James Publishing. Morgan James and The Entrepreneurial Publisher are trademarks of Morgan James, LLC. www.MorganJamesPublishing.com

The Morgan James Speakers Group can bring authors to your live event. For more information or to book an event visit The Morgan James Speakers Group at www.TheMorganJamesSpeakersGroup.com.

Shelfie

A **free** eBook edition is available
with the purchase of this print book.

9781630478490   paperback
9781630478506   eBook
9781630478513   casebound

Library of Congress Control
Number: 2015917348

CLEARLY PRINT YOUR NAME ABOVE IN UPPER CASE
Instructions to claim your free eBook edition:
1. Download the Shelfie app for Android or iOS
2. Write your name in **UPPER CASE** above
3. Use the Shelfie app to submit a photo
4. Download your eBook to any device

Cover Design by:
Rachel Lopez
www.r2cdesign.com

Interior Design by:
Brittany Bondar

Editor: Deb Haggerty

To Susan:

The love of my life, who started this journey with me in college and married me following graduation in 1976. We've had an incredible journey that has given us a wonderful son, Richard, a daughter-in-law, Kelly, and two adorable grandchildren, Makayla and Richard. Our singing ministry has taken us around the world and provided us these heart-warming stories to share. As the journey continues, I want to say thank you for standing by my side and always being there for me. I love you.

Table of Contents

ACKNOWLEDGEMENTS

I would like to say "Thank You" to Deb Haggerty for her countless hours of hard work in consulting, editing, proofing, and retyping these short stories. Our family is honored to call her our friend. I have had the privilege of working with her for over twenty-five years. Her expertise, professionalism, and knowledge have been priceless in writing and compiling this book.

Thanks, Deb, for all you've done to help with this book and for encouraging me to have *Joy for the Journey* published. I never could have done this without you.

Chapel Valley Studios have been our recording studio almost from the start. Shane, Travis—we are ever so grateful for your talents and abilities to make our CDs sound great. Shane, we also thank you for all the wonderful songs you have written for us to sing. We appreciate all of you.

I'd also like to thank the rest of my family for putting up with me when I'm on deadline and for giving me such great material for this book. Richard, Kelly, Makayla, Richard—you give me great *Joy for the Journey.*

Most of all I want to thank my Lord and Savior, Jesus Christ, who graciously gives all of us *Joy for the Journey.*

· JOY FOR THE JOURNEY ·

The Lord wants to give us an abundant life filled with joy and peace. Scripture tells us: *I came that they may have and enjoy life, and have it in abundance (to the full, till it overflows)* (John 10:10 Amplified Version). Our lives can be hectic, but we don't want to miss the God sightings—to see God working in all of our life situations.

Our family, The Hyssongs, (pronounced "his-songs." Yes, that really is our last name) travel full time singing southern gospel music. We do about two hundred fifty concerts a year traveling up and down the Eastern US and into Canada. We've seen God doing great and mighty things during our journeys and trust these stories will be an encouragement to each of you.

After traveling three hours one Sunday afternoon, we finally arrived at the church where we were scheduled to sing. After quickly setting up and doing a sound check, we went out to our motorhome to get dressed. After everyone was ready, we gathered in the front of the bus for prayer like we always do.

We entered the service but could never have imagined what God was about to do. This was not going to be just another meeting; we were going to be meeting with Almighty God. As we started singing, several people on one side of the church started to get up. I thought to myself, *don't leave now we are doing the best that we can.* They weren't leaving—they were going across the aisle hugging, crying, shaking hands, and getting right with God and each other. The Lord had used a song to touch several people. Apparently there had been a real division in the church. Revival broke out that night and we just kept singing. We had sung about three more songs before they sat back down.

The next thing that happened was the icing on the cake. From three rows back, a teenage boy got up from his seat and came forward and knelt down on the step just below me. Three men got up and came to the front to pray with this teen. That young man was accepting Jesus Christ as his personal Savior. Wow! I have to wonder if he realized that the people in that church were real and genuine and not hypocrites. When he saw them getting right with God, he knew Christianity was not just a religion, but rather a personal relationship with Jesus Christ.

Great joy was everywhere that night—joy in the church, joy in the family that saw their teenage son give his life to Christ, and joy for our family who had the opportunity to see God at work in a miraculous way.

God will meet us where we are and when we need Him. You never know when He will show His presence. Until next time, don't miss God at work in your life and remember that God wants you to have *Joy for the Journey.*

• The Cost of Freedom •

In May, we take time to honor those who have served our country in the military and to remember those who have given their lives to protect the freedoms we enjoy here in the United States. My dad is a World War II veteran and was wounded in 1945 fighting in Germany. I was raised to be patriotic and to be proud of our flag, the national anthem, and this great country of ours that God has blessed so much. I am not ashamed to tell you that my eyes still fill up with tears when I go to a Memorial Day parade, hear the bands play, and see the stars and stripes of Old Glory coming down Main Street.

Last year our journeys took us to a church on Memorial Day Sunday. We will never forget our experience there. While we were setting up our equipment, the pastor entered the sanctuary on crutches. One of his legs was obviously missing, but you hardly noticed because he had such a sweet spirit and positive Christ-like attitude.

The pastor shared with us that his leg had been badly injured during the Vietnam War. A buddy of his had rushed back to his aid after he had been wounded, put a tourniquet on his leg to stop the bleeding, and then had to move out with the rest of the troops. His friend assumed that the pastor would never survive his injury.

However, the pastor did survive—after spending months and months in hospitals and rehabilitation centers. God had spared his life, but for what purpose? The man had not been a Christian when he was injured. Not until after the war did he accept Christ as his Savior and then accept God's call to become a pastor. So you see he was saved not once but twice: once physically and once spiritually.

For almost thirty years the man who tied the tourniquet around the wounded leg thought his friend must have died. Imagine his surprise when they met years later at a military reunion.

The Sunday morning we were scheduled to sing, the pastor's friend had flown across the country to visit and attend the church. As the time of the service grew closer, there was a feeling of excitement and anticipation in the air.

After we sang "America the Beautiful" and "God Bless the USA," a man from the congregation spontaneously stood up and asked if all those who had served in the military could stand up front so everyone could thank them for their service to our country. There were hugs, tears, and appreciation shown that day. The whole church was thankful not only for all their veterans but also for the man visiting that day who had saved their pastor's life.

Let's remember to say thanks to those who have served and are serving our country today. I trust each of you will continue to have *Joy for the Journey* and may God continue to bless the USA.

• ALMOST PERSUADED •

Some people will come to a concert who would never come to church. That gives the gospel singer a great responsibility and opportunity to witness.

Several years ago, our family sang and shared in a wonderful church. As we closed the concert, I invited people to accept Christ. No one responded and I must confess I was a little disappointed.

After the service, I was at the door shaking hands. An older gentleman stopped and said, "You almost got me tonight." I replied by saying, "You almost accepted Christ tonight?" He said, "Yes." I encouraged the man to join me in the pastor's office. I wanted to tell him about salvation again and give him another chance to make that great decision. The man looked at me and said, "Not tonight."

The pastor of the church was standing close by. I got his attention and explained the situation. The pastor offered the same opportunity saying, "Roy, your wife and family have been praying for you for years. Why not accept the Lord today?"

The man opened the door, headed down the front walk, and called back over his shoulder, "Not tonight." The preacher asked if he could stop by his home and the man surprisingly replied, "Yes." The pastor told him he would be there on Tuesday.

We packed up our equipment and drove out of the parking lot with hearts burdened for a man who needed Christ.

A few weeks later we received a letter from the pastor. The second paragraph said, "I also wanted you to know I visited with Roy the following week and was able to lead him to Christ. We have been praying for him for over twenty years. Thank you for your part in faithfully sowing the seed."

I tucked that letter in my Bible and often get it out to remind me that God's timing is perfect and that we all have the responsibility to pray and sow the seed.

The pastor finished his letter to us by writing, "continue to sing for Jesus (I know you will), and, Lord willing, we will see you next fall."

A few months ago, we returned to that church. We talked about Roy in the motorhome and wondered if he'd be there that night. The church was packed and a whole row was filled with Roy's wife, son, and family. His son thanked us for our part in Roy's salvation and told us his father had died just two days before. He said, "It's hard for us to be here tonight, but we didn't want to miss this concert and the opportunity to thank you. We know Dad is in heaven." The family asked us to sing "Amazing Grace" during the concert because it was Roy's favorite. What a time we had as we celebrated Roy's home going and sang that great hymn together.

Friends, we wouldn't have missed that opportunity to go back. What will God do next time? There is *Joy for the Journey!*

· A Thief in the Night ·

I like to find a front-row parking space when I go to the mall or a grocery store. In fact, I've been known to circle a few times waiting for the perfect spot only to have someone pull in just ahead of me—can you relate?

We always hope to pull into a church or concert hall parking lot with our motorhome and find a parking place close to the door of the auditorium, so we don't have to lug our equipment very far.

One Sunday night our desire became a reality. A door about six feet away led onto the platform where we would be setting up and singing. We couldn't expect anything better!

Following the concert that night, my son, Richard, went out to the motorhome to quickly grab something that he had forgotten. When he came back inside the church, his face was ghost-white. He looked at me and said, "I must have closed the motorhome door too hard because the glass all shattered." We rushed out to see what had happened and discovered something far worse. While we had been singing, someone had used a glass cutter to cut the window, reach in to unlock the door, and rifle through our entire motorhome. They stole wallets, pocketbooks, cash from the entire weekend, Bibles, tax returns, future recording arrangements, and so much more.

Our hearts seemed to stop beating, and I must confess I was in total shock from all the mess, the loss, and most of all the invasion of privacy.

The next hour or more involved talking to the sheriff, cleaning up all the shattered glass, and canceling credit cards. We had lost just about everything.

God took action that night and proved to us that He was in control and that He could provide.

Before the concert, we had filled our tank with diesel so we knew that we could travel through the night. Within twenty-four hours, we had new credit cards delivered to the studio in Nashville where we were recording. A church heard about the robbery and immediately sent money through Western Union. (By the way, all of our ID was stolen, so WU accepted the pictures on a CD cover as proof of our identity). Our home bank issued new account numbers and changed all of our passwords, etc. Our insurance company replaced pocketbooks, wallets, Bibles, and the expense of new driver's licenses.

In fact, when everything was all settled, God had supplied twice the amount that we had lost.

At the Department of Motor Vehicles, we did not have enough identification to replace the stolen licenses. We stepped up to the window and a clerk whom we'd never seen before said, "I'm sorry to hear about your robbery." After telling her about our lack of the necessary identification she said, "That's okay, I'll be your witness." Do you suppose she was an angel? Only the Lord knows! But one thing is for sure, God always gives *Joy for the Journey.*

· A Meeting with Almighty God ·

Probably some of your favorite groups go on gospel-singing cruises where passengers can sign up to hear wonderful gospel music—a super way to spend your vacation! You see lots of new places, spend time with some of your favorite artists, and hear great gospel music. You only have to unpack once, and everything comes at one affordable price.

A few months ago we had the privilege of singing on a cruise to Alaska. When we boarded the ship in Seattle, I never imagined the beauty and splendor that we were going to see and the wonderful things that would happen. The snow-capped mountains, icebergs, glaciers, bald eagles, and whales were all breathtaking. The food, fellowship, and music were great, too—although I must confess that I ate a little too much at the delicious meals which were served on the ship.

Without a doubt, the best part of the cruise was Sunday morning. The cruise line opened their large theater and invited all of the gospel groups on board to sing. I was asked to preach the sermon. The passengers on board to hear gospel music and the singers themselves had only a portion of the ship's cabins, so I wondered if any of the other passengers would come to the service. That morning hundreds of people started to flood through the doors and they filled the auditorium. I was so excited! I prayed and asked the Lord to do something very special that day.

Each one of the groups sang, including our family, and then I opened the Word of God. I shared how we ought to live in these last days before Christ returns. At the end of my sermon, I described how people could accept Christ as their personal Savior and led them in the sinner's prayer.

The response was phenomenal. We had people stopping us on the ship, in the dining hall, and even when they saw us walking in Juneau and Skagway, to tell us of decisions they had made in that service. Some people shared how they had prayed to accept Jesus Christ. One couple told us that they had not been in church for years and they'd made a commitment to go back to church when they returned home. A husband and wife talked to me about a cult that they belonged to, which they were going to leave now and told me that God had changed their lives that day. God had given us a wonderful opportunity to share Christ's message of salvation. Sunday was not just another sermon; it was a meeting with Almighty God.

I don't know why I doubted that anyone would come to the service that morning. The Lord had something very special planned all along. He brought in the people that He wanted to be there, and He worked in their hearts and lives. A simple gospel cruise turned into a wonderful opportunity to share Jesus, and again the Lord gave us *Joy for the Journey.*

• THANKFUL •

R ecently I saw a plaque that read: "faith, family, and friends—for these we give thanks." I am thankful for many things and praise the Lord for this Thanksgiving.

I am thankful for my salvation. As one songwriter penned, "without Him, I would be nothing." I praise the Lord for my family. I am always mindful of the love and support they give me. I am also thankful for the opportunity to serve Jesus. What a privilege to travel and proclaim the good news of Jesus Christ through song. Even more exciting for us is to see God challenge and change lives.

A couple of months ago we were invited to minister at a Family Bible Camp for a weekend of singing and preaching. We would have less than a day and a half to travel over fourteen hundred and fifty miles. They wanted us to sing at the meetings, preach three messages, and end the weekend with a full concert. After inviting us to come, they told us what they could afford to pay. The money was not even enough to cover our diesel, but I felt we should accept the invitation. I learned many years ago it's not the money or mileage that matters, but people's lives. If we do what God wants, He will take care of us and supply our needs. That is His promise, and He always keeps His promises—one more thing for which I am thankful.

The Thursday arrived when we were to leave. We left home early that morning to sing at a state fair before starting the 1450-mile-long journey. We had a long, uneventful trip and thirty hours later we arrived at the family camp.

The meetings and concert went great, but the best part was yet to come on Sunday night. They'd planned a campfire with songs, a devotional, and testimonies. That night, under the beautiful starlit sky, people began to share what the weekend had meant to them. A teenage boy stood by the fire and told how the messages and songs had brought him to surrender his life to pastor and preach the gospel. God is so awesome!

How tired or weary we were, or how far we were from home, that boy reminded us again that people's lives are what really matter. Perhaps he'll be another Billy Sunday, D.L. Moody, or Billy Graham. Whatever he becomes, I'm thankful that God used us and that we drove those many miles to invest in his life.

Maybe you are a pastor, Sunday school teacher, or sing in the church choir—no matter how weary you may be—don't quit or give up. You never know what a difference you are making in lives. There may not be a campfire or time for you to hear the results of your labor, but God knows and is working through you.

Let's remember to thank Him not only on Thanksgiving but all year long as He gives us *Joy for the Journey.*

• CHRISTMAS MIRACLE •

C hristmas is one of the most magical times of the year. The decorations, lights, laughter, and the aroma of our favorite foods cooking in the kitchen are all a part of this special day. All these things are great as long as we keep in mind that we are celebrating the birthday of our Lord and Savior Jesus Christ.

The familiar song, "I'll Be Home for Christmas," is true for our family and something we look forward to each year. We may not be home for birthdays, anniversaries, or other holidays, but we always find our way home for Christmas.

We have recorded several Christmas CDs including our newest one called *Christmas*. Churches frequently call to ask if we can sing and preach during the Christmas season. We gladly accept as long as we can get home by Christmas morning.

One Christmas Eve we sang and shared at a Candlelight service. That evening will be etched in my mind for a long time to come. The decorations were absolutely beautiful. There were green garlands hung on the pews, candelabras lit on the platform, and candles lining the center aisle.

People filled the church that night, and you could sense the festive spirit and excitement in the air as praises were sung to celebrate the birthday of the King. The service concluded with everyone singing "Silent Night" while they held lighted candles. Then I prayed and wished everyone a Merry Christmas.

As I stood by the door greeting folks as they left, a young man in his early thirties shook my hand and wished me a Merry Christmas. He stepped out onto the porch and disappeared into the cold, dark, snowy night.

I finished greeting the rest of the people as they left the church. After everyone seemingly was gone, I turned around and hurried back into the sanctuary to help my wife and son pack up our equipment. Just then, that young man opened the door and reappeared. He asked if he could sit down and talk for a minute. Although this was Christmas Eve, and we were anxious to get on the road and head home, we are never too busy to talk, pray, or minister to someone in need.

Right then and there I had the privilege of sharing Christ and leading Carl to the Lord. He had heard the message of a Savior, who was born. He had learned how the cradle led to the cross and one day a crown. Carl realized his need that night for a Savior and was gloriously saved.

On the first Christmas, I can only imagine how the angels sang and rejoiced when Jesus was born. I can just imagine on this night all the angels in heaven singing and rejoicing over Carl being born again.

There was *Joy for the Journey* on the way home for us that night, and I know that there was joy for Carl, who had come to realize the love of Christ that Christmas Eve.

· I WILL TRUST HIM ·

The start of the New Year is a great time for new beginnings. People make resolutions and plan anything from saving money, dieting, and paying off credit card bills to being better spouses, parents, and even Christians. I can't imagine how many things are going to be promised this New Year again as we make a fresh start.

Most resolutions will be broken very quickly because they are being made without considering God. In John 15:5, Jesus says *for apart from me you can do nothing* (New American Standard Bible).

Just think what we can do *with* the Lord. Philippians 4:13 says, *I can do all things through Christ who strengthens me.*

Our family does not make resolutions; however, we do resolve to renew our commitment each year to serve the Lord. Our desire is to be used of God and to live for Him.

When we come to the end of the year, we are excited to look back and see how God has used a sermon, a song, or a recording to touch someone's life. This month I would like to tell you three short stories that brought us joy during this last year.

One teenager told us how his car had broken down in a deserted area. It was a cold, dark night, and he walked to the nearest house to get help. He was scared to knock on the door until he looked through the window and saw one of our CDs sitting on the window sill. He said, "I knew if they had your music, I would be safe." Those folks helped him that night by calling his parents and a wrecker. Can you imagine that God had them place the CD right there on the window sill that night for a frightened teenager to see?

Last Christmas when many families gathered together for the holidays, a man sat alone in his home. His wife had left him and taken the children with her. He told us that he played one of our CDs and heard the song, "I Will Trust Him." We had tears in our eyes when he said, "I just kept playing that song over and over all day long. It got me through the hardest day of my life."

Another family emailed us to say that they had been called to Philadelphia when a family member had been rushed to the hospital. They stayed at the Intensive Care Unit around the clock. They wrote to tell us that each day around lunch time, they would go out in the car and listen to our music and pray. After a long illness, their loved one recovered. They were rejoicing that God healed her and used our music to lift their spirits and help them through a very difficult time.

As we approach a new year, there will be many resolutions, but I am more interested in allowing God to continue to use us and to keep giving us *Joy for the Journey.*

· HAVE IT GOD'S WAY ·

ulltime gospel singers find themselves living more on the road
than at their homes. Traveling becomes a way of life and sometimes we forget how much we've been away until we come home
and find a major change has occurred.

Recently we came home and discovered that our neighbors had
moved out and a new couple had moved into the house across the
street. We were only going to be home for a day and then gone
for the weekend. I decided to wait until we returned home to go
across the street to meet our new neighbors. After all, we really
wanted to welcome them and help them feel at home in our community. After singing three concerts, we finally were returning
home for a few days. We were driving down our street when all of
sudden I saw the ugliest mailbox in their front yard.

Even though I write a monthly article called *Joy for the Journey*, I
confess that their ugly mailbox gave me a bad attitude and robbed
my joy for a time. I wondered at our new neighbors' bad taste.

That night I went to bed and as I was trying to sleep, I discovered
that they not only had an ugly mailbox, but they also had a dog
that yipped and yipped all night. The next day I was ready to talk
with our new neighbors about the mailbox and dog.

My time came when I saw the man coming down his driveway. I
walked up my driveway and we met by the side of the road. I'm
glad I let him speak first. He shook my hand and said, "We're new
in the area. My wife and I have been excited to meet you because

I heard that you preach and sing gospel music. I work with someone who knows you and lent me some of your CDs. We don't go to church anywhere, but I wondered if you were singing in the area if it would be alright for us to come and hear you." I'm so glad that the Holy Spirit shut my mouth. I would have wrecked any chance I had to share Christ with them.

Sometimes we seem to want to have our way instead of God's way. We'd rather win a fight than win someone to Christ.

I've never mentioned the mailbox or the dog, but I have mentioned the Lord and our concerts several times. I have a burning desire to lead this couple to Christ. You see, I not only want them to feel at home in their new neighborhood, I want them to be saved and feel at home with the family of God.

When my focus changed, and I adjusted my attitude, I again felt joy. Mailboxes, dogs, or whatever bothers you or me are only temporary. Real joy comes when we set our eyes and affections on eternal things. May we always be concerned about God's will and have *Joy for the Journey*.

• Patience Pays •

Today when people want instant oatmeal, instant grits, instant potatoes, instant coffee, etc., the Lord still works in His time. Most of us need to learn patience and to wait on the Lord. Noah took a hundred twenty years to build the ark. God prepared Moses for eighty years before he led the children of Israel out of Egypt. We need to remember God's timing is perfect and always best.

Several years ago our family was driving down the highway when suddenly lights on the dashboard illuminated. They indicated the water was low and that the engine was going to shut down. We pulled off the road, got out to see what the problem was, and discovered a huge fan blade had gone through the radiator. No wonder the water was low; it was pouring out on the ground.

Our motorhome was towed to a garage where a couple of weeks passed waiting for new parts and a radiator. During those weeks, I talked with the service manager by phone many times and came to know him on a first-name basis.

When I finally picked up the motor home, the service manager said, "I hope you don't mind, but I saw one of your CDs on the dashboard and decided to listen to it." I assured him that I didn't mind, thanked him for his service, paid the bill, and drove away, never expecting see him again.

Two years later we were setting up our equipment on a Sunday morning and who should come through the door? You guessed right—the service manager. He walked up to shake my hand saying, "You probably don't remember me." I told him I did and even called him by name. He said he had grown up in the area and was back visiting his mother. I later learned that he had been raised in the church, but had walked away from God and his heritage. His mother had prayed for him for years and that morning everyone was excited to see him back.

We haven't seen him since, but in December his mother came to our product table at yet another concert to tell us *the rest of the story.* Apparently her two sons had not spoken to each other for over ten years. Something had come between them, ruined their relationship, and broken their mother's heart.

She was beaming with joy as she told us how both her adult sons had been at our concert two years before. She said, "That concert changed my boys' lives! That day they spoke to each other for the first time after all those years. Now they talk all the time!"

Only God could have orchestrated these two brothers being at the same church service that day. God used a hole in our radiator five years previously to begin answering a mother's prayer and healing a broken family, but the results weren't instant. When we wait on His timing, God surely brings *Joy for the Journey.*

· ALARMING ALARMS ·

In these busy days, people seem numb to alarms going off. In fact, most of us barely take a second look when car horns start beeping and lights flash on and off in the parking lot. The other day we were in the mall when an alarm began sounding. Everyone seemed to go about their business except one man who asked the clerk what the alarm was. Alarms seem to go unnoticed.

However, our family has set off a few alarms this year that have drawn quite a bit of attention.

Recently we were the last people leaving a church. The pastor told us to set their security alarm when we were packed and ready to leave. After we loaded our equipment, my son, Richard, thought everyone was outside, so he stopped, set the alarm, and exited the building.

Not long after that, he realized that his wife, Kelly, was still inside. She had stopped in the ladies' room and when she came out, she tripped the motion detectors. We could see her panicked face through the glass doors. She didn't know the code or what she to do. She opened the door to let Richard in so he could shut off the alarm, but it was too late.

The church telephone began ringing, and Richard reluctantly answered it. The man on the line asked if everything was alright and what the password was for the church. Fortunately, we had been there before and they had told us what the password was in case the alarm was ever set off. Unfortunately, they had changed the password during the year, and Richard kept giving the wrong word.

Only a few short minutes passed before the police arrived—lights flashing. After many long minutes, we finally got everything straightened out and were allowed to leave.

You would think that we had learned our lesson. Oh, no. Just a few months ago, we arrived at a church early. We tried the doors; one was open, so we thought someone had left the door open just for us. Wrong ... they had set the alarm and forgotten to lock the door.

We went in, and the alarm began to blare so deafeningly loud. There was no way to turn the alarm off, so we just started carrying in our equipment. Shortly after, a policeman arrived and stood there with his hand on his gun while we continued to carry things into the church until the pastor arrived.

You've seen our pictures on this book cover. Do we look like criminals? Maybe you shouldn't answer that! The pastor and the church had a good chuckle at our expense that night. We've sure learned to pay attention to alarms!

Each time we were surprised and startled when the alarms went off. I wonder if we will be as surprised when the trumpet of the Lord sounds. I believe we will hear that blaring sound very soon, and we then will certainly have *Joy for the Journey*.

• Precious Memories •

I will never forget my mother's voice calling me for supper when I was a boy or sitting next to her in church while she gave me Life Savers to keep me quiet. These memories will be in my mind forever and I will always be thankful for our talks and her prayers for me through the years.

Mother's Day is a great time to honor our mothers and remember that God gave them to us.

A couple of months ago during one of our concerts, we sang the old hymn, "In the Garden." While we were singing, a lady took a piece of paper and wrote us a note that she handed to my wife at the end of the singing.

Susan tucked the note aside; we packed up our equipment and started down the highway before she remembered to get the note out and read it to us.

Here's what the woman wrote: "Thank you for singing the old hymn, "In the Garden"—it was my mother's favorite hymn. I remember her playing the piano and singing when I was just a little girl. Recently my mom became seriously ill and was in the hospital. One day while I was visiting her, the doctor came in to tell me there was nothing more they could do for her and that the time had come to unplug the machines. I climbed up on the bed, laid down beside her, put my arm around her, and soaked her with my tears as I tried to choke out the words to that beautiful old hymn. I was trying to sing her favorite hymn to her when she took her last breath. Thank you for singing "In the Garden" for me and my mom tonight."

That note has certainly reminded me that every time we sing, we need to be aware there are hurting hearts in the pews. It also is a wonderful tribute to a mother that was loved by her daughter.

This year Mother's Day falls on May 11, 2008. I hope we will all take time to tell our mothers we love them. For those whose mothers are no longer here, I hope you'll take a few minutes to remember them.

The Bible tells us to *Honor your father and your mother.* We are to observe this all year long—not just one day a year.

In two months, I will become a grandfather for the first time. My son and daughter-in-law are expecting a little girl. We are all very excited as you can only imagine. I know Kelly is going to be a great mother, and we love her. I'd like to take this opportunity to say Happy Mother's Day to my mom, Carolee; the mother of my son, Susan; and Kelly, the mother-to-be. I would also like to wish all of the readers who are moms a wonderful day. Mothering can be a challenge, but the task also brings great pride and *Joy for the Journey.*

• GODLY HERITAGE •

T he other day I stopped to visit my mom and dad. They had been cleaning out some closets and decided they wanted to give me some of the family heirlooms.

Our family has always enjoyed passing things down from generation to generation, but the most priceless thing that has been passed down to us is a love for God. Handing down family heirlooms is great, but God's Word tells the Israelites and each one of us what is far greater to pass along.

Deuteronomy 6:4-7 says *Hear, O Israel: the Lord our God the Lord is one! You shall love the Lord your God with all your heart, with all your soul, and with all your might. And these words, which I command you today, shall be in your heart; you shall teach them diligently to your children, and shall talk of them when you sit in your house, when you walk by the way, when you lie down, and when you rise up.*

These verses are a wonderful reminder of what all dads and moms ought to strive to do for and with their children and grandchildren.

Last summer, on a warm Sunday morning, our family sang in a country church to a crowd of gospel music lovers. When the concert was over and people were leaving, an older lady asked if Richard and I would sign her Bible. The Book was worn and tattered and she opened it carefully to the inside cover. She told us that she had asked people to sign her Bible, who had made a difference in her life over the years. I was humbled as I took her Bible and wrote my signature under the few names that were there. When I passed the Bible to Richard, he looked at the list of people who had made a difference in her life and at the top of the list he saw his great-grandfather's name. My grandfather had been her pastor in the early 1940s. We stared at the name in amazement as we praised the Lord for our godly heritage and the circumstances that had brought us and the woman together.

I will always cherish and hold dear the heirlooms that my parents have passed down to me. Years from now, I will pass those treasured things down to my son and his family. The most important thing passed down to me from my father and grandfather is their faith and knowledge of how to have a personal relationship with Jesus Christ—a faith I've passed down to Richard to continue their legacy.

I don't know if I'll ever see that lady and her Bible again, but they sure gave us Joy for the Journey on a warm summer day.

I often wonder what our great-grandchildren will hear and say about us in the future. Let's make a commitment to teaching our children and grandchildren to follow the Lord.

Happy Father's Day! I pray that each of you know *Joy for the Journey.*

· LOOKING ON THE LIGHT SIDE ·

Most of us remember hearing while we were in school that "no question is a dumb question." Lately, I've questioned that statement as I find myself asking some of those questions.

We've had people ask us things that have made us chuckle. The Bible tells us that *a merry heart does good, like medicine ...* (Prov. 17:22). So these questions have been good medicine for us. They've given us a lot of laughter during our journeys. I hope they will brighten your day too.

One Sunday night, we were standing behind our product table before the service. Our CDs were displayed on several racks and a large backdrop was up behind us with our name in large letters. A person came up to us and asked, "Oh, are you singing here tonight?" Now I really wanted to reply, "No, we set all of this up for fun." Then someone else asked, "Are you the singers tonight?" I wanted to say the singers just let us put our pictures on the CDs, but to both questions, we just smiled and said yes.

People always seem fascinated with groups' buses and motorhomes. We are very thankful that God has provided us a vehicle to travel in from concert to concert, but we get some strange questions. Recently someone asked, "Do all of you travel and sleep in that?" As there are only six of us, I so wanted to say, "No, Richard rides on the roof" or "I stuff him in one of the bins." Again the Lord helped me to be gracious and bite my tongue.

Not long ago, my wife was asked, "How do you do laundry and

ironing?" You have probably guessed—we go to laundromats while we are on the road unless pastors' wives and friends allow us to use their laundry rooms.

Probably one of my favorite odd situations was when we arrived to set up at a church. Richard was wearing his jeans and t-shirt. We set up quickly and ran out to our motorhome to get changed. When Richard returned in his suit, a man stopped him and asked him where his brother had gone. The man was convinced that Richard must have had a twin brother and we could not convince him otherwise.

We are not laughing at these people, but we do find some of the questions we get to be humorous. Sometimes I stick my foot in my mouth, but I'm glad to report the Holy Spirit mostly keeps my mouth closed so I haven't given many of the answers that popped into my head.

Friends, laughter, and a merry heart are good medicine and sometimes we laugh so hard going down the road that we almost cry. The questions we are asked can be humorous or sometimes very serious, but they all bring us great joy.

I hope you too can look on the brighter side of life. We try to do so as laughter gives us *Joy for the Journey.*

• Making a Difference •

One July 4th weekend, we sang at a patriotic concert outdoors. The summer evening was beautiful and the crowd was lively and energetic. They sang along with the entertainers and cheered for Christ and our country.

After the concert was over, I picked up a couple of our speakers and started to take them to the motorhome. I can't express how happy I was when I glanced back and realized two men had also picked up some of our equipment and were following me. We always appreciate when people will help us lug equipment out to the motorhome after a concert.

As I started putting the gear in the storage compartments, one man said to the other, "Have I ever told you how I got saved? A friend of mine had to die so I could live." He continued to tell about a friend he had at work who used to talk with him about the Lord and about salvation. He mentioned his friend's name (let's call him James) and said, "One day, James told us he had been diagnosed with cancer. Even though he was struggling with cancer treatments, he continued to share his faith at work."

The man's story caught my attention because I used to be James' pastor—that's what I did before being called into our full-time music ministry. So I listened intently as the man continued to tell the story about his friend whom I also knew.

He said, "James eventually died from the cancer and I went to the funeral service. As Dell spoke about James and shared about his love for the Lord, I gave my heart and life to Jesus Christ."

I continued to listen quietly and humbly as the man was sharing his testimony and also letting me know in a subtle way the part I had played in his salvation several years ago.

He said, "I accepted Jesus Christ into my life, was baptized, and joined the church. Today I'm active in my church, have a weekend music ministry, and tell others about the Lord—all because of a faithful, godly man who witnessed to me at work."

When James died at such a young age leaving a wife, children, and loved ones, we were saddened deeply. Often times we wonder and question God about many things in life we don't understand, but James' legacy lives on through the man who claims that his friend had to die so he could live.

I knew the man who died and I believe James would tell us, if he were here today, that he'd suffer cancer and die all over again if someone would be saved because of it. That's the way he was. Isn't that exactly what Jesus did for us? He willingly went to the cross for all of us. He had to die so we can live.

We should all share our faith openly with family and friends. Leading someone to Christ gives us surpassing *Joy for the Journey*.

• HUNG UP •

Early one November, our family was traveling to a church where they were planning a concert and harvest dinner. We had been discussing our family Thanksgiving plans and talking about all that we had to be thankful for as a ministry and family.

When we arrived at the church, I needed to turn and go up a steep driveway. As I made the turn to go up the hill, the back end of the coach started to drag and before I knew it—we were stuck. The back frame of the motorhome was hung up on the crown of the road with the rest of the vehicle partly up the steep driveway—we were very stuck.

Our thankfulness turned to concern and we asked the same question many of you ask—why? Why was God allowing this to happen?

Within a couple of minutes, two policemen were directing traffic because we were blocking the street and only one lane was open. They had called a wrecker to come and help, but we learned he could not get to us for at least an hour.

I was standing near the back of the coach talking with the police corporal as he directed traffic when suddenly he said, "I know you. My wife and I attended a concert when you sang with Russ Taff." Another officer took over as he continued to talk with me. He had lots of questions and finally asked where I had grown up. His eyes widened when I told him because my hometown was his too. He had graduated from the same high school as I one year earlier.

The wrecker finally arrived, pulled us out, and the driver said, "That will be one hundred dollars." Would you believe my dad had given me a one hundred dollar bill just before we left on this trip?

I started the engine, which sounded terrible. However, we managed to coax the engine to give enough to get around the block into the rear entrance to the church.

Just before the concert, the policeman showed up in plain clothes with an old high school yearbook. He told me he had asked a mechanic friend to stop by and look at our engine. We checked out the old pictures and laughed at the way we looked back in high school. We enjoyed talking about friends we had in common and the activities we'd taken part in. I couldn't believe that during this mishap, and so many miles away, I'd met someone from my hometown who was there to help.

In the middle of the concert that night, I was handed a note that read, "Bus fixed! =$0."

I may not know why God allowed our misadventure to happen, but once again I can say, "Thank you, Lord! I'm glad You are in control." Seeing Alan and learning that he is saved was great. Knowing that the Lord always takes care of us is wonderful and gives us *Joy for the Journey*.

• Celebrate Joy •

We are getting ready to celebrate Christmas, which is without a doubt my favorite time of year. For some people, however, the season is difficult and even depressing. Some people are struggling with our economy and reduced paychecks. Some have recently lost loved ones and are mourning. Some folks are hurting from broken families and relationships. Looking at the trimmings and decorations and trying to conjure up some kind of warm and fuzzy feelings does not work for them even though the world places great emphasis on these things. Real joy at Christmas or any other time only comes from the Lord.

The songwriter, Isaac Watts, penned the words, "Joy to the World, the Lord is Come!" The fact that our Savior was born should bring us great joy. To use an old cliché for this special day, we should focus on the reason for the season. People keep their focus on Jesus in many ways. Some people read Scripture, others make a birthday cake for Jesus, and some donate to a ministry or give a gift to a needy person or family. Only a true celebration of Jesus' birth brings us real joy.

Our family will sing on Christmas Eve again this year. We will be about an hour from home, so after we finish and pack up, you know where we'll be heading. All the way to the house, I'll be singing "I'll Be Home for Christmas." I'm like a kid on Christmas Eve. We'll read the story from Luke 2—*I bring you good tidings of great joy which will be to all people. For there is born to you this day in the city of David a Savior, who is Christ the Lord.*

Christmas morning all the family will gather at our house to exchange gifts and sit down to a big meal. We'll talk, laugh, and share lots of stories together. Like some of you, I always picture that our celebration is going to be a combination of Norman Rockwell and the Walton's, but we are just an average family. Our table might not look like the spreads in the fancy magazines, but we have the Joy of Christ as we celebrate His birthday.

A few years ago when Christmas fell on Sunday morning, we had a service at our home church. Following the Christmas celebration, I was shaking hands and asking an elderly lady where she was going for dinner. She said she was going home for leftovers. She told me that she didn't have any living family members. A couple of hours later she was sitting at our table as we became her family for the day. She has since gone home to be with the Lord. This Christmas she has been reunited with her family and enjoying the family of God.

I look forward to sharing many more stories about our travels in the months to come, but until then, we wish you a very Merry Christmas and *Joy for the Journey.*

• Life Stinks •

I hear from folks sometimes, "life stinks." As I'm an optimist, I have a hard time relating to that statement. Last week, however, we had two separate incidents that caused me to say, "This stinks."

Early Monday morning I was driving through Tennessee when I looked ahead and saw a skunk crossing the road. My wife was sitting up front with me while the rest of the family was asleep in the back. I said, "It'll be okay, he's heading for the other side and I'll miss him." As the words left my mouth, the skunk turned around and walked right under the motor home. I now know what people mean when they say "life stinks."

A couple of hours later, after the rest of the family got up, they said, "Do you smell that skunk?" I said, "Smell him? I hit him!" Believe me, I heard about the skunk and smelled him all day.

To have one skunk story in a lifetime would be enough, but I had two in one week.

Three days later we were in Sharps Chapel, Tennessee, having a barbecue on the patio with some friends. We'd just finished eating and were enjoying the fellowship when my wife urged me to get up slowly and move toward her. As I did, she told me there was a skunk less than two feet behind me. My body might have been moving away from him slowly, but, believe me, my mind wanted to get me out of there fast!

As we all crept toward the house, our host ran inside and emerged with a shotgun. He said. "Don't worry, I'll hit the skunk in the head—there won't be any smell at all." Those famous last words will echo in my mind for a long, long time. Why is it when someone says not to worry, it is exactly the time to worry?

He fired three shots and surprise! The "odor" sack was hit. I have never smelled anything so bad in all my life.

We headed back to the motor home with the smell that permeated our clothing coming right along with us. Now we had skunk smell on a tire from Monday and skunk smell inside the motor home from the clothes we were wearing. Right then I could say, "Life stinks" literally!

I couldn't help thinking as we journeyed with that stench that many people take their bad attitudes and problems with them. Life doesn't stink. Our attitudes may, but life is what we make of it. The Lord wants to give us victory and joy, but sometimes we refuse the gift.

We've had a lot of laughs this week about our two skunk episodes. I know that people who think "life stinks" aren't talking about the same thing; but I'm hoping if any of them are reading this article, they will stop looking at their problems as "stinking" and start looking to the Lord—allowing Him to give them *Joy for the Journey*.

· The Worth of a Soul—Priceless! ·

Diesel fuel is four dollars and fifty cents a gallon, a gallon of milk almost five dollars, the worth of a soul—priceless! Obviously, I borrowed the idea from a credit card commercial, but that's why our family and so many others continue to travel across America with great joy proclaiming the gospel of Jesus Christ.

A few weeks ago, we had the opportunity to minister at a church that had three Sunday morning worship services. Between the eight-thirty and nine forty-five a.m. services, my son, Richard, stepped outside to get a breath of fresh air.

A car pulled into the parking lot and two boys emerged from the back seat. Their mother rolled down her window and beckoned for Richard to come over. She said, "I am a Buddhist, but I had a strong feeling that my two boys needed to be in this church today. My oldest boy doesn't see the point in being in any church; would you sit down and explain the reasons to him?"

With that, she drove away leaving her twelve- and eight-year-old boys standing there with my son. Richard invited them to come into the church. They followed him into the foyer where Susan and I were standing by our product table. He quickly explained what had happened. I looked at the boys and said, "We are going to be singing this morning so why don't you come and sit with us.

The song leader had already started the second service as we all walked down the side aisle to sit in the front row. When we got up to sing, the boys watched and listened intently. I was excited anticipating what God would do in their young lives.

Following the service, the pastor's wife came to say that she taught a boys' Sunday school class during the third morning service and the boys could go with her.

When we finished the last service, the pastor's wife came back into the sanctuary, her face beaming, to tell us about her class of boys. She said, "Usually the boys are very talkative and sometimes they fool around. Today they were so quiet that I had a chance to present the clear gospel message of salvation. But best of all those two boys both accepted Jesus Christ as their personal Savior."

I would love to have been in the car to hear their answers to the question, "Do you know what the point of going to church is now?" when their mother came to get them.

The pastor and his wife are following up with the family. Our prayer is that all of them will come to a saving knowledge of Jesus Christ and that they would discover serving and knowing the living God.

The cost of living is rising fast, and some people seem to be nervous and scared. But even with life's uncertainties, the cost of a soul is priceless! God is still in control, and there is always *Joy for the Journey*.

• WHAT GOES AROUND COMES AROUND •

The golden rule says, "Do unto others as you would have them do unto you." We all have heard this rule and know that we should apply it every day. Matthew 25:40 reads, *Verily I say unto you, Inasmuch as ye have done it unto one of the least of these my brethren, ye have done it unto me.* (King James Version) Treating others with kindness and respect is a Biblical truth that is often ignored.

In 2003, my wife was asked if she would be the substitute teacher for a fourteen-year-old boy who had autism. His regular teacher had been in an automobile accident and was going to be out of school for several months. Our schedule allowed Susan to fill in for a few weeks and so she accepted the challenge.

We would sing on weekends and then she poured her life into this young man at school from Monday through Friday. Her teaching was so successful his parents went to the school officials and requested that Susan be hired as his full-time teacher. She had to turn the offer down because we were getting ready to leave for a three-month tour.

Sometimes people come in and out of our lives, and we never know why. Often we think about people in our past and wonder where they are today. Recently we found out exactly why God had brought that boy into our lives.

On July 19, 2008, at 4:44 a.m., our son and his wife had a beautiful baby girl. We had sung the night before and got home two hours before they went to the hospital.

All of our joy quickly turned to concern when some health issues were discovered. Her heart didn't sound right, so the hospital called the pediatrician who was on call for the weekend to come in and examine her. When the doctor arrived, she asked Richard if his mother was the singer. He confirmed to her that our family sings.

The doctor said, "Five years ago your mother substitute taught for my son. She was so good to him and helped him so much. Tell her that he is doing well and is in college now. I came right away to take care of your baby because your mom took such good care of my son." She finished by saying, "What goes around, comes around."

When Richard called us from the hospital to tell us what had happened, we just thanked God for His goodness to us.

Treating someone with respect and kindness five years ago meant that our granddaughter got some very special care and attention today.

My granddaughter still needs a lot of prayers, but we have a great God, and we are trusting Him and His power to heal and care for her.

Did I mention that this is my first grandchild? That means I've got pictures. She is so precious and gives us such joy. Even in the midst of trials, God gives *Joy for the Journey.*

• CHANGES AND CHALLENGES •

The New Year will bring changes and challenges for many of us. Our family always uses this time to reflect on the past and to seek God's wisdom and guidance for the future. We are entering into this New Year with excitement and anticipation. Looking forward, we are excited to serve the Lord and to anticipate what He is going to do among His people.

Looking back, there are a few things, however, that we'd like to forget. We are often asked what our most embarrassing moment has been. Believe me we've had many.

In September, we were at the National Quartet Convention, where there are always lots of Christian television and radio stations represented. We have fun catching up with DJs and television hosts whom we have gotten to know over the years. We really appreciate their hard work and devotion as they spread the Gospel through music and the Word through this very special means of communication.

Late one night we were told that the next evening we were scheduled for a television interview. The next afternoon we confirmed with our friend the time and place of the taping.

We got all dressed up and greeted people on the convention floor while we waited for our scheduled appointment. When the time came, we went to the booth that was set aside for taping. The lady with the appointment book looked at us and then back at her book before finally telling us that we were not on her schedule.

Richard assured her that we were definitely scheduled, and perhaps someone had forgotten to write our names down. Fortunately for us, a former singer with another group recognized us and greeted us with hugs. We had done a couple of concerts together and he knew us from those days. He had left the road and now worked with this television network.

The scheduler said she was sorry for the mix-up and got us right on the set for our interview. Everything went great and we finished our time by signing release forms and saying our good-byes.

As we were leaving, we saw the editor of *Christian Voice Magazine*, John Lanier, standing at the *Gospel Music Television* booth with a microphone in his hand. Our hearts sank a little and I must confess that my face turned red as I wondered if we had done the right television interview. We were so insistent that they had made a mistake.

We walked toward John and asked if he was expecting us. He replied, "I've been waiting for you and you are fifteen minutes late."

I was embarrassed, to say the least. I relied on the verse that tells us God always works everything for good. And I'm resting on Philippians 3:13 that tells us *forgetting those things which are behind, and reaching forth unto those things which are before* (KJV).

As we enter the New Year, let's keep our eyes on Jesus, have a happy one, and *Joy for the Journey*.

• Prayers Needed •

In July, 2008, I became a grandfather for the first time. I cannot begin to tell you the love, joy, and sheer delight our granddaughter has been in these first years of her life, but the real love story is what God has been doing.

As I was sitting in the waiting room with my wife and our in-laws, Richard called from the delivery room to announce her arrival. "She's here and she doesn't look anything like you, Dad." I thought *I've been up all night to hear this?* Then he said, "She doesn't look anything like you—she has hair!" On July 19th at 4:44 a.m., Makayla Hyssong was born.

The next two days were filled with laughter and joy as we took turns holding her and taking the usual pictures. We were also busy because we had to leave to sing that night as well as the next day. Richard was racing between concerts and the hospital as only he could do.

Forty-eight hours later the pediatrician examined the baby before discharging her from the hospital. He listened to her little heart and said, "I hear something that could possibly be a heart murmur. I'd sleep better tonight and so would you if she went to a larger hospital for an ultrasound."

After taking his wife, Kelly, and daughter, Makayla, home from the hospital, Richard drove four hours to meet up with us for some more concerts. The next day, Makayla was scheduled to see a cardiac specialist. That afternoon we received a phone call that was totally unexpected. Makayla did not have a heart murmur, but instead they had found twenty small tumors in and around her heart. One was blocking the blood flow and was life-threatening if it grew larger.

All of our laughter and joy turned to tears and concern as we headed home to face a very grave situation. The doctor had said that these tumors could shrink in a couple of years, but they usually grow larger first. He allowed her to go home, but would do an ultrasound every two weeks.

We were so thankful for people all over the country who started to pray for us and my little granddaughter.

When she was thirteen days old, there were more ultrasounds and tests. That night the doctor called Richard and Kelly to say that the tumors were just as serious and he was sorry to inform them they had also found some brain tumors. The next few days and weeks were filled with ultrasounds, MRIs, and appointments with multiple specialists. Our song listed on the radio charts, "God is There," became more real to us and meant more to us than our audiences could ever imagine.

People were praying, God was working in our lives, and the Lord was bringing *Joy for the Journey* in the midst of a difficult situation. To hear the rest of Makayla's story and the tale of her miraculous journey and God's love, read Part II next.

· Prayers Answered ·

Previously, I started to tell you about my granddaughter, Makayla, born on July 19, 2008. She entered this world and the world has not been the same since. Three days after her birth, the doctors discovered twenty small tumors in and around her heart. One was significantly blocking the blood flow in her heart and was life-threatening if it enlarged. At thirteen days old, she was diagnosed with brain tumors too.

Would she survive? How would the brain tumors affect her development? We kept praying and people all over the country began praying. She had ultrasounds every two weeks, an MRI, blood tests, and more doctor appointments than I'll probably ever have in my lifetime.

When she was fourteen and a half weeks old, the pediatric cardiologist listened to her heart and said, "I don't hear the swishing noise." An ultrasound revealed that the blood was flowing adequately and the heart was beating normally for the first time.

The doctors had told us that if the tumors were going to get smaller, the process would take at least two years. Yet the ultrasound showed the tumor blocking the blood flow had started to shrink already! Don't tell me that there is no God! Don't tell me that God doesn't answer prayer! And don't tell me that God doesn't give joy for our journey. We saw a miracle.

That same day, Makayla saw the neurologist. The MRI of her brain certainly did not seem to him to match what he saw in my granddaughter. She was smiling, cooing, and very alert. He looked at her and said, "I don't understand—she is developing perfectly normally for her age."

The doctors may not be able to understand, but we do. God is the Great Physician, who hears His people's prayers and answers in miraculous ways. We don't know what tomorrow holds, but we certainly know Who holds tomorrow.

Richard asked the doctor, "Should we just keep praying for her?" He replied, "That seems to be working, yes, keep doing that."

Makayla is alert, she's growing, and she's healthy. I can't wait for you to see her at one of our upcoming concerts. She has been cleared to travel with us and we are enjoying her every minute.

To answer many of your questions, let me say yes, I have pictures, I love being married to a grandmother, and I'd have had a grandchild first if I had known how wonderful they were.

I love the words that Bill Gaither penned about the sweetness of holding a newborn baby and knowing that whatever happened in their lives would be fine because He lives.

Friends, I've opened my heart these last two months and have told you a love story—not a story about our family, but rather a love story about God and what He has done for us and Makayla. I thank so many of you for praying and thank God for His love and for giving us *Joy for the Journey.*

• WOUNDED WARRIOR RETURNS •

On March 3, 1945, as the 4th infantry division of the US Army pushed into Germany, one of our heroic soldiers felt a burning sting run down his back before he lost consciousness. He'd been hit by a bullet from heavy German fire.

Lying in a ditch, he regained enough consciousness to hear the medics picking up the wounded and leaving the deceased. He had no idea how much time had passed. When they reached his motionless body, he heard one say, "He's dead—we'll leave him." Right then God gave him the strength to pick up his head enough to turn to the other side and groan.

Two German POWs picked him up and carried him back about a block to a small village. From there he was placed in a jeep with other wounded soldiers to move him back from the front lines. He later found out the jeep was the last one out that day because of heavy artillery fire.

His wounds required months of surgeries, hospitals, and rehabilitation before he was well enough and strong enough to travel home. A surgeon said the bullet was only a quarter of an inch from his spine. Just a little further and he would have been paralyzed or worse.

Back home, his parents and fiancée waited to hear some word from their loved one. The letters had stopped, and they knew that something had happened. Their fears were realized when they received word from the US Army that their loved one had been wounded in action. "How bad was he? Where was he? Will we ever see him again?"

The soldier had a visit from a chaplain. He offered to write a letter back home for the soldier because he was unable to write at that time. So from his hospital bed in Luxemburg, he began to dictate the letter that all of his loved ones at home were waiting to receive.

He did come home fifteen months later. He was wounded and broken, but proud to have served his country and glad to be home with a family that loved him. Fifteen days after returning to the US, he married his fiancée. The soldier that I'm proud to write about is my dad and his fiancée—my mom.

If you were to ask him if it was a coincidence that the bullet stopped a quarter of an inch from his spine, or if it was lucky that he woke up to hear the medics pass by, he'd be quick to give God all of the credit, honor, and glory. It's not luck or coincidence—it's God.

Many men and women have not come home from wars we've fought. On this Memorial Day, we have an opportunity to remember them.

Let's never forget the sacrifices that have been made to keep us free. Today, because of those who have served our country in days gone by, and those who are serving now, we can have *Joy for the Journey*.

· We Saw the Light ·

Following our concert, a man rushed past our product table saying, "I've got to go home and get some money, I'll be back." He slipped out the door and, going the opposite direction from the parking lot, disappeared into the woods. He emerged again a bit later with some money and purchased three of our CDs.

While we were packing up our equipment, the man came back and asked one of the men from the church, John, if he would help him fix a light in his house. The man was legally blind and could not see to fix the chain that had broken on his light fixture when he went to get his money. John said he'd fix it in the morning, but we could tell by the expression on the man's face that he needed help then.

I told John we would be glad to come along if he'd do the job that night. I grabbed a flashlight and the three of us followed the man into the woods.

Walking through the dark woods, we came to a clearing containing a small out building. He opened the padlocked door, pushed a burlap sack aside, and we entered the room. The rustic shed had a bed, table, toilet, and sink, but there was no heat or air-conditioning. Obviously the man was one step above homeless.

The light in the middle of the room had a chain to turn it on and off. The chain was broken and couldn't be fixed that night because a whole new fixture was needed.

John said he'd take him to the hardware store the next day. He would help him get the light working, but the cost would probably be about ten dollars. The poor man said he thought he had enough money to buy what was needed, but he wasn't sure. Richard and I exchanged glances because we knew he had used his money to buy our CDs.

Before we said goodnight, the man said, "I do pencil drawings. If you send a picture of your granddaughter to the church, they can give it to me, and I'll draw her picture for free."

Talk about the widow's mite! This man had nothing, but he was willing to give everything. He might be poor materially, but he is rich spiritually.

We walked through the woods and back to the church in total silence. Standing in front of the church, John told us that he would take the man to the hardware store in the morning and attach a new fixture to the ceiling for him. Richard and I reached into our pockets and gave John the money to purchase the new light.

Just when we wonder how we will survive the difficult economy, someone else comes along to show us how blessed we really are.

Acts 20:35 says, *It is more blessed to give than to receive.* Being able to help that man and purchase his new light brought us *Joy for the Journey*.

• Now is the Moment •

How many times have we heard the saying, "don't put off until tomorrow what you can do today?" The Bible tells us that we have no guarantee of being here tomorrow. *Today or tomorrow we will go to such and such a city, spend a year there, buy and sell, and make a profit; whereas you do not know what will happen tomorrow. For what is your life? It is even a vapor, that appears for a little time, and then vanishes away.* (James 4:13b-14) Despite that, many people procrastinate and put things off.

In January, a husband and wife came to one of our concerts and sat in the front row. The very next day the husband called to tell us they would like to come on our gospel singing cruise that was sailing in just two weeks.

The couple signed up, came on the cruise, and had the time of their lives. They enjoyed the music, the fellowship, the food, and all the ports. On the final day of our cruise, they came to me and showed me a beautiful ring that the man had bought for his wife. He even told me that I would buy something for my wife if I weren't so cheap. After six days, I guess he thought he knew me well. I'm really not cheap—I'm just frugal and conservative.

A week after the cruise was over, and everyone had returned home, I received an email from one of their friends. The note told us how happy they were that their friends had come on the cruise with us. For years, they had been praying for this couple, and when the couple had returned home from the cruise, their lives had been changed. During the concerts and chapels, they had both accepted Jesus Christ into their lives.

I was so excited to read this email until I came to the last paragraph. The email went on to say that a few days after the cruise, they were driving down the highway when the husband had a severe stroke, drove off the road, hit a tree, and was killed.

Can you imagine if he had decided to put off the cruise until the next year? Worse yet, what if he had decided to wait awhile until he accepted Christ? Procrastination would have changed a happy ending into a tragic one. The happy ending that I write about is his eternal destination of heaven. I'm not making light of the stroke or the accident. I know that all of the family have had a difficult time, but I also know that his timely decisions have brought much comfort and joy.

By the way, his buying the ring for his wife will also give her wonderful memories of a husband who loved her so very much.

Tomorrow is not promised to any of us. Therefore, we ought to live for God and make the right decisions for Him today to have *Joy for the Journey.*

• IT IS WELL WITH MY SOUL •

The crispness in the air, the changed colors of the leaves, the shorter days—all of these things signal fall has arrived. Each year at Thanksgiving, we always take time to thank God for His many blessings. However, the meaning of blessings changed for me recently.

I was greeting people coming in for a concert when a young man in his thirties rolled through the door in a wheelchair. I walked toward him and reached out to shake his hand. He introduced me to his father who was pushing the wheelchair and the three of us started a conversation.

The young man told me about the accident that had left him paralyzed. He said, "I was twenty-three, had a great job, and was engaged to be married. We had had a snow storm and I got on a plastic flying saucer to slide down a hill. As I was speeding down the hill, a tree jumped out in front of me, and I crashed into it and broke my neck."

He told me about the months he spent in a rehabilitation hospital and also shared how he lost his job, his fiancée, and the ability to ever walk again. Yet he said, "I know the Lord, I'm blessed, and I've never been depressed about this."

I stood there and listened as he praised the Lord for his salvation. We laughed together as he told me how he had skydived from an airplane recently, strapped to an expert, and parachuted down to the earth.

Here was a young man who had seemingly lost everything, yet he was praising the Lord because Jesus was all that he needed. His story was a solemn reminder that we have so much to be thankful for this Thanksgiving.

We started the concert. The fourth song we sang was the hymn, "It is Well with My Soul." On the chorus, I looked back at my new friend and I could see him mouthing the words from his wheelchair—"It is well, it is well with my soul." My son sang the last verse and I lifted my trumpet to play the last chorus of the song. I was so filled with emotion, I was not sure I could finish.

Tears streamed down my cheeks as I observed a man who could be complaining, but instead was praising God and giving thanks. What a testimony that young man is to his community, church, and each of us! Peace, joy, and contentment from God are far better than anything this old world can give.

We who know the Lord are so blessed. Let's stop mumbling, grumbling, and complaining, and start praising God for all that he has done for us and promises to do for us in the future.

Have a wonderful Thanksgiving. Enjoy your families and the bountiful food, but most of all—rejoice in the faith that you have in the Savior. Remember happiness and thanksgiving are choices. I hope you'll choose *Joy for the Journey.*

• The Greatest Gift! •

The lights on the tree were sparkling so colorfully on that Christmas Eve. Under the tree was an old Lionel train set that my father had had as a child. The train ran around a village that was perfectly displayed. There were smells of pies cooking in the kitchen. We were all happy as we anticipated the presents we'd open in the morning and visits from the family. Like memories are for many of you, this childhood memory is vivid for me. I remember that I'd seen a Danny O'Day dummy in a catalog and I wanted the toy very badly. I'd even been practicing my ventriloquism just in case I got Danny. Even with all the practice, I still couldn't talk without moving my lips—I still can't today, though I certainly do plenty of talking.

Later that night, when time to get ready for bed arrived, my mother first helped me get some cookies out for Santa and place them neatly on a plate.

I went to bed but had a hard time getting to sleep. A child's mind can really play tricks on them when they're waiting for a sleigh to land on the roof. Little did I know that my parents worked into the early morning hours putting toys together and getting them all wrapped.

If I had known, maybe I wouldn't have jumped out of bed at four thirty a.m. to wake up my parents and sister. They were all good sports and got up so we could go downstairs to open our presents that were under the tree. The plate was empty with only a few crumbs and Santa had certainly left us lots of presents.

One of the last gifts handed to me was a box wrapped in colorful Christmas paper with a red bow on the top. As I ripped it open, there was Danny O'Day. I picked him up and started pulling the string to make his mouth move. The problem was that my mouth moved along with Danny's.

I'll never forget that Christmas. By the way, my father's train set, then eighty-four years old, is still in a box in our closet. The train still runs and is something we treasure. Danny O'Day hasn't been played with for many years, but he too lies in a trunk at our home.

This year we are still making memories. We are decorating our home, sending out cards, exchanging gifts, and spending time with the family. Today we focus not on Santa, but on our Savior. Today is His Birthday and I am waiting for Him to come again. I happen to think He'll be coming very soon.

When I think of all the gifts that I have received, they pale in comparison to the greatest gift that God has given us—His Son, Jesus Christ.

Our family would like to wish you a very Merry Christmas. If you remember the reason for the season, you too will have *Joy for the Journey*.

· Nothing is Impossible! ·

Happy New Year! Weren't we just worrying about Y2K yesterday? How can we already be greeting another year? However, people are still worrying about things. When will we realize worrying won't change anything—God is still in control?

In October, two things happened that not only brought us joy but also reminded us of the fact that God is still on the throne.

One Friday, FedEx delivered a package of product to us. We stored the box under our motorhome and left for a weekend of four concerts. Following the Sunday night concert, we headed for home in the dark and rain. I don't know how long we'd been driving before we realized that a bin under the motorhome was open. We pulled over and got out to see what had happened. The latch had broken and allowed the door to fly open. My heart sank when I realized the product we had just received was gone. We had no idea how many miles back the box had fallen out or what condition our product would be in if we went back to look. So we temporarily fixed the latch and decided to continue on toward home.

On Monday morning, I made a call to reorder the product hoping that we could get the shipment in time for our next concert.

On Tuesday morning, I was at my desk when the phone rang. On the line was a FedEx driver saying, "Someone found a FedEx box and all the contents scattered over the road. The person gathered the contents and called me to come get them. Did you ever receive this package?" He assumed the box had fallen off a FedEx truck and never been delivered. I answered, "I received the box last Friday," then proceeded to tell him the story.

The driver told me the tracking number was still on the box along with our address and that all the items seemed to be in good condition. They would deliver the package the next day. I inquired about the charge. He replied, "Because you were honest—nothing. The delivery will be free."

By the way, let me tell you what also happened that same Sunday night.

As we were setting up, a young couple came to talk with us. They excitedly told us they had been praying for their neighbors for the last three years and, as far as they knew, the neighbors had never been in any church in their lives. However, their neighbors had agreed to come to church with them that night!

To make a long story short—the neighbors did come. Before the night ended, the wife gave her life to Christ. Now we are praying for her husband. He has said he is going to start attending the church.

God is still in control and He demonstrates that to us every day. As we welcome the New Year, may you be happy and may you allow God to give you *Joy for the Journey.*

• AWKWARD TUMBLE •

One December, we were watching three couples participate in a version of the Not-So-Newlywed game. I'm always amazed at the answers people give when they are in front of an audience. The final question to the women was, "When would your husband say that he last embarrassed you?"

I looked at my wife and she looked back at me. I knew exactly what she would answer had we been sitting up there. Thankfully we were not participating because she would have told everyone what had occurred the night before.

Here's what happened: I was about to go on stage to start a gospel concert. The doors had opened at six thirty p.m. to lines of people anticipating hearing the concert and their favorite groups. At seven p.m., I was to give a welcome to the people and introduce the first group. As I ran up the two steps to the platform, my foot caught on the top step, I stumbled out on the stage, and awkwardly tumbled to the floor.

There was some snickering. One person shouted, "That was graceful!" Other people were horrified and remained silent as they watched to see if I would or could get back up. My wife, who was standing backstage, looked concerned for me and a bit embarrassed at my entrance.

As I stood up, I tried to pretend everything was all right. I could feel blood running down my leg, but had no idea my pants leg had ripped across the knee. By then, the audience could see that I was hurting. The Bible says in Proverbs 16:18, *Pride goes before destruction, and a haughty spirit before a fall.* In my case, after the fall. I'd definitely lost all pride and dignity and was humiliated and embarrassed. Considering what happened, everything else was fine. I went on to introduce the first group—we had another great night of gospel music.

Having a tumble like that at any time is embarrassing but in front of an audience?! Strange how falling is embarrassing even when we could and often do get hurt. Susan better not bring my fall up again, especially as Valentine's Day is just around the corner.

Once again on February 14th, many of us will be scrambling to buy flowers, candy, or something special for the one we love. Susan and I have been married for more than thirty-five years, but I still want her to feel very special on Valentine's Day. They say it's really not the gift or amount that we spend, but rather that it's the thought that counts. If that is true, then she really must know how much she is loved. She has to know I'd never embarrass her on purpose, but we've certainly laughed about my fall since that night.

Don't forget the one you love on Valentine's Day, but keep your first love, Jesus Christ, close to your heart so that your footsteps don't falter and so that you can have *Joy for the Journey.*

• MUSIC IS UNIVERSAL •

Music has often been said to be the universal language. Music can play an important part in bringing people to Christ and moving others to life-changing decisions.

I stood in a Ukrainian church in 1991, and sang "How Great Thou Art" only to hear almost a thousand people sing along with me in Russian. I've seen altars filled and people weeping following a gospel concert. Once I even saw people in a church that was hurting and splitting spontaneously move from their seats and start seeking forgiveness from each other during a song. Hearts were moved and a mini-revival broke out that day.

Music can challenge and change people and cause them to be tender-hearted toward the things of God.

In December, I received an email that once again reminded me that music is universal and crosses many barriers. David wrote:

> My wife interprets for a deaf woman who has started to attend our church, and who, although she was raised in an atmosphere where she had been taken to VBS as a child, never understood anything about God because she was deaf and no one took the time to help her understand.
>
> During your concert, your son brought his daughter up on the stage. The deaf woman was moved to tears when he shared how God still answers prayer.
>
> She loves music and can experience the vibrations (that

aspect some older church members tend to fuss about). She has since made a profession of Salvation. The very first thing that she expressed after her salvation was that she wants to sing for God using her hands as a voice. She will be *singing* to the Lord at our talent night next Saturday.

Just wanted you to know that your *sound* ministry has influenced even those who cannot hear with its *sound* doctrine of faith!

As I read the email over and over, I praised God for his love and the gift of music that can reach everyone. God can reach across language barriers and hearing obstacles or anything else to bring people to himself.

God's Word instructs, *be filled with the Spirit, speaking to one another in psalms and hymns and spiritual songs, singing and making melody in your heart to the Lord* (Eph 5:18-19)

Many times we rush by people who speak a different language. I'm sure I've been guilty of ignoring a deaf person because I've either been embarrassed that I couldn't communicate or fearful that they would not understand me. Next time I'm going to pay more attention, stop to shake hands, talk to them through an interpreter, or just give them a smile.

That deaf lady will now be able to reach a group of people that I'd perhaps never be able to reach. I'm happy she felt the vibrations and *heard* what we said and sang through that interpreter.

She now makes melodies in her heart to the Lord. Like those of us who know Christ, she will now have *Joy for the Journey*.

• Obstacles vs. Opportunities •

Life on the road is very exciting for our family. We love seeing God working in the hearts and lives of people. Many people today look at the obstacles, but we look at the opportunities—and the opportunities are great.

While many focus on the economy, the jobless rate, earthquakes, Iran, Iraq, and Afghanistan, we look to Jesus. I believe these things are a sign the King will be coming before long. If you agree with me, then you'll also agree that we need to get busy because there are many lost people who need to be won to the Lord.

During the winter of 2009, we had the opportunity and privilege of sharing the gospel message in word and song in a Florida church. Now that's not new for us since we sing close to two hundred fifty concerts each year, but that morning a couple attended. The husband responded that morning by accepting Christ and the wife responded by rejecting Christ.

Recently, we were invited back to that same church. The couple doesn't attend there, but they came to see and hear us once again. The wife still had not accepted the Lord, but a lady there had been encouraging her and helping her throughout this last year. The lady has helped her take care of a loved one who has health problems, provided transportation, and invited her to Bible studies and other gospel sings.

Our family prayed as we always do before going into the service. We asked God to challenge and change lives. We also prayed that the wife of that man would come and be responsive to the Lord's leading.

When the time came for me to give the invitation following our concert, ten people responded. I was humbled by the response, but the person who caught my attention was that man's wife. She raised her hand indicating that she wanted to accept Christ and then leaned over toward her husband and whispered to him. I could read her lips as she said, "I prayed that prayer." He nodded and smiled and a sweet peace came over him.

I stood there trying to finish the service as tears flowed down my cheeks. This couple has not only spent their lives together as husband and wife, but they will also be spending eternity together with the Lord.

The woman who has been helping them spoke to me after the concert and said, "I've been praying for and encouraging that woman all year long. Now I'm going to disciple her and help her in her Christian walk and life."

Sometimes driving all night, eating at a greasy truck stop, paying the high price of fuel, and breaking down on the highway can seem like obstacles, but they're a small price to pay for all the opportunities that God brings our way.

I'm thankful that both this husband and his wife have new life in Christ and I'm also thankful that He gives us *Joy for the Journey*.

· IMITATING GOD ·

Traveling full time and singing over two hundred fifty concerts each year as a family has challenges because we share a motorhome, but that is another story. Believe me, the joy of spending so much time with my wife, son, daughter-in-law, granddaughter, and grandson far outweighs the challenges.

When my granddaughter, Makayla, was twenty months old, she constantly imitated everything we did or said. You can imagine that although those imitations could be good, her imitating us could also be very bad.

Several years ago, when we were being introduced by a pastor, I couldn't count how many times he said, "Amen." Each time he said the word, you could hear Makayla's little voice saying, "Amen" from the back pew. You might laugh and people around her did smile and laugh, but Richard wanted to crawl under the pew each time she imitated that preacher.

When we set up and do our sound check, my granddaughter often will pick up a microphone and stand between her dad and me and sing right along with us. Do you think that I'm proud of her and spoil her just a little bit? That's what grandpas are for, isn't it?

On another day, we were driving and noticed a pair of Richard's shoes was in the aisle of the motorhome. Yes, we trained him better than that, but what can we do now? We looked up and saw Makayla standing with both feet in one shoe. I don't know how she got both her feet in the shoe, but we knew she couldn't get out by herself.

She obviously wanted to walk in her Daddy's shoes. That is why setting a good example for her is so important. Our lives are the Bible that she reads, so we need to make sure she sees Jesus in us.

This month is Mothers' Day and next month is both Grandparents' Day and Fathers' Day. We have a responsibility and the wonderful joy of setting an example before our children and grandchildren. They are watching and imitating us.

Makayla still makes us laugh and is sweet as she imitates us, but we know what she sees and hears to imitate is serious, because she is going to grow into the kind of young lady that we train her to be.

By the way, just as she imitates us, we should be imitating God. Ephesians 5:1 says, *Therefore be imitators of God as dear children.*

Probably we make God laugh with our feeble attempts to imitate Him. But as we grow in the knowledge of the Lord and His Word, we will become children of God who please Him.

Traveling with my family and doing what God has called us to do brings great joy into my life. Imitating God and being who he wants me to be gives me even greater joy. We need to laugh, enjoy our families, be in the Word, and imitate God. These things will certainly give us *Joy for the Journey.*

• NOTHING TO WHINE ABOUT •

Sometimes the slightest inconveniences can irritate us and cause us to lose our focus and purpose in life.

One May, my son and I had the privilege of going to El Salvador with Compassion, International, to see the great work they are doing with children in that country.

I boarded the plane and sat down. The chair back and tray table in front of me were wrapped in duct tape. The words written on the tape were simple: *Broken—do not use.* I must confess I thought if the tray table is broken, where do I put my Coke? I also wondered what else might be broken that I couldn't see.

Looking around, I realized I was sitting in front of the emergency doors over the wing and my seat was securely fastened in the upright position. I couldn't tip the seat back for my in-flight nap.

Our flight included a change of planes in Chicago. We circled the airport for more than forty-five minutes because of storms in the area. By the time we landed and got to the gate, I was sure we had missed our connecting flight. As we were running through the airport to our next gate, I glanced up at the monitors. Not to worry, our next flight was delayed for four hours.

I'm sure that we can all agree that inconveniences can irritate all of us.

Sixteen hours after stepping off the plane in El Salvador, I was standing by our product table following a concert and noticed a husband and wife coming toward me. He was obviously blind and held her arm as she led the way.

They stopped to talk for a minute, then she left him by me as she went to look at our music. We talked and every once in a while he would lean toward me and touch his shoulder against mine. I'm sure he wanted the security that someone was still there for him.

I thought to myself of my recent inconveniences and all of them paled in comparison. I certainly have nothing to whine and complain about.

Then the man said something I will never forget. He asked, "Do you know what my favorite song is?" While I pondered his question, he answered, "What a Day That Will Be When My Jesus I Shall See." He continued by saying, "He will be the first one I see and I can't wait!"

If that doesn't put things into perspective and cause us to get our focus and purpose in life back on Jesus and off ourselves, nothing will.

I put my Coke on my son's tray, slept sitting up, and got to my destination on time. The little bumps in life should never cause us to lose our joy. Let's keep our eyes on Jesus and remember our purpose is to live for Him and glorify Him.

We shall see Him face to face before long. So until then, may we all have *Joy for the Journey.*

· CALL 911 ·

Several years ago someone died during our concert. I will never forget all that took place that night and I'm sure the audience will never forget what happened either.

Could such a thing occur a second time? During a concert recently, as I glanced out of the corner of my eye, I saw a lady looking very gray. Suddenly she leaned to one side and slid down in the pew toward the person next to her.

Let me tell you, to keep singing when someone is yelling for a nurse, someone else is asking for an ambulance to be called, and the family is wailing, is very difficult.

We did what all of you would do and stopped singing. I wanted to pray for the lady, but before I could say anything, the pastor went into panic mode. He had never had this happen before and he decided to ask everyone to leave the building. He told the audience to evacuate the auditorium to leave room for the paramedics. The pastor was so rattled he didn't realize that when he told everyone to leave, they would hinder and block the paramedics both in the hallway and the parking lot.

The nurses in the church were working on the woman and people were scrambling to leave. Richard and I walked to the back of the church. Richard looked at me and said, "She is dead." I certainly agreed with him after seeing her, the CPR being performed, and the reaction of the family.

However, a few minutes later I looked back into the auditorium and she was standing up. I looked back at Richard and said, "If she was dead, there's been a miracle because she is standing up." The ambulance attendants made her lie down on the stretcher and told her she needed to go to the hospital to be checked out.

They wheeled her out the door to the ambulance and finished preparations for the ride to the hospital. They lingered long enough that I decided to go out and pray with her before they took her away.

After I had prayed, she started to insist she be allowed to go back into the church. Her concerned grandchildren told her she need-ed to go to the hospital and asked why she wanted to go back in. She told them that she had come to buy our CD and she was going to buy one before we left. A grandson told her, "Grandma, you go to the hospital and we'll buy you a CD."

I need to say that the lady is doing just fine. She apparently had a bad spell and fainted.

What was learned that day? The pastor told us he won't panic if a similar situation occurs. God provided for us like He always does. A family is thankful for a mom and grandmother who is still alive. And finally, we all were reminded that time is short and we need to have *Joy for the Journey*.

· A Little Rain Must Fall ·

We've all heard the expression that into every life a little rain must fall. Another familiar expression is when it rains it pours. A little rain isn't bad, but recently we had a day when all the heavens opened up and we had a downpour like you'd never believe.

Friday night we sang in a high school auditorium. After the performance we were all tired, so we decided to sleep there in the parking lot in our motor home. When we got up on Saturday morning to go to our next concert, I started the diesel engine and the stoplight flashed on. That's never a good light to see. When the light has appeared in the past, the onboard computer has actually turned off and shut down the engine.

However, everything sounded okay and the computer allowed me to keep driving. Fortunately, we were only two hours from home so I decided to drive slowly home, repack all the equipment into our trailer, and use the van to travel to our next booking.

While I was driving, someone decided to use the computer to find a motel for the next night. When they tried to boot up the computer, nothing happened. The air card that we have had for years to connect to the Internet apparently wasn't working.

Now the motor home was broken and the computer card was also broken. What else could possibly go wrong? Finding out didn't take very long.

We finally got home. I quickly hooked up the trailer to the van and started to pull up the driveway. My wife called out to me to get out and check the trailer tire because there was a huge bubble on the edge. I knew the tire wouldn't last many miles.

We changed the tire and were finally on our way again. An hour down the road we decided to pull off at an exit because the telephone store was there and we could either fix or get a new air card for the computer.

While we sat on an overpass waiting for the traffic light to change, railroad gates came down several car lengths ahead of us. However, there was a problem because a pickup truck was there on the tracks with nowhere to go. A nineteen-year-old girl flung open the door, leaped out, and ran to safety just before the train made impact.

No one was hurt, but do you have any idea how long clearing that kind of accident takes? We couldn't turn around or budge an inch. There we sat until they moved the train and a tow truck came to pick up the truck.

We made our concert and got a story to write, but what a day! Enough rain showered down on my life during those twenty-four hours, I thought I should build an ark like Noah. However, another song says that the sun will come out tomorrow! During the rainy and sunny times, God always gives *Joy for the Journey*.

• Boats and Planes •

Frustration and disappointment are a part of life. Although all of us would probably agree, they are not the parts we enjoy.

Our family had been invited to perform on a gospel-singing cruise to Alaska in July. We planned, anticipated, and looked forward to once again visiting that awesomely beautiful state. The day before our cruise departure, we were to fly from Portland, Maine, to Newark, New Jersey, and then on to Seattle, Washington. Our early morning check-in went smoothly. We were told the flight was on time, but soon discovered it was delayed. We were getting anxious because we had little time to make connections in Newark. Suddenly our anxiousness turned to frustration when the flight was canceled.

Everyone scheduled on that flight crowded up to the ticket counter seeking other flights. Finally, we were told they would pay for us to take a bus to Boston, fly from there to Philadelphia, and catch a connection to Seattle.

We raced downstairs to get our luggage off the carousel and grabbed a taxi across town to the bus terminal. We arrived in Boston with plenty of time to check-in again, get through security, and even to grab a burger on our way to the departure gate. We were glad to finally be on our way, but our enthusiasm was soon dashed after the plane pulled to the side of the runway and shut down its engines. The pilot announced there were storms in Philadelphia and we were going to sit at least an hour.

We held on to the hope that maybe our connecting flight would also be late because of the storms. Finally after landing in Philadelphia, we ran through two terminals only to reach our next plane in time to see them close the door in front of us. That night we slept in the terminal with the promise of flying to Phoenix, Arizona, in the morning.

When morning came, we boarded the plane and as soon as the plane had pushed back from the gate, all the engines shut down. The pilot said, "The luggage doors are shut, but a light is on in the cockpit and must be fixed before we leave." We finally took off, but with little hope of arriving at the cruise ship before it sailed.

Lest I frustrate you any further, we made the next connection and as we were landing in Seattle, a young man sitting next to me said, "I work downtown close to the docks. My car is here at the airport. Can I give you a ride to the ship?" I don't know if he was an angel, but to us he was. We were the last passengers to board the cruise ship.

An eight-hour trip turned into thirty-two hours, but in spite of it all, we had a great week of ministry on the cruise. We can go through life frustrated by glitches and delays, or we can enjoy the journey. I choose *Joy for the Journey*.

· Good News or Bad News ·

You've heard the saying, "do you want the good news or the bad news?" The bad news is we stopped for diesel on a recent trip to Ohio. I'm not talking about the price of diesel, but rather an incident, which happened that night, I'll never forget.

My wife, Susan, took the credit card and headed out the door to prepay the fuel. She turned around and asked our granddaughter if she wanted to come along. Makayla jumped into her arms and off they went.

I had just started to pump the diesel when I heard a loud noise and saw smoke billowing out everywhere. I dropped the hose and started pounding on the motor home while running for safety. My daughter-in-law, Kelly, and son, Richard, jumped out of the motorhome. They could not see anything but smoke. Kelly ran to the front of the motorhome screaming for me while Richard crawled on the ground searching for me because they could not hear or find me. Finally, they heard me screaming from the other side of the motorhome.

A trucker had revved up his engine and the exhaust pipes on top of his rig sparked, which caused the overhead fire extinguisher to go off. The powdery chemical that violently gushed out from the extinguishers covered us as well as the inside and outside of the motorhome. The EMTs washed out our eyes with saline because they were red and burning from the chemical. Richard and I suffered immediately from upper respiratory problems and became very hoarse from inhaling the chemicals.

The bad news is that our health was affected, the motorhome was a mess, and we were forced to cancel four dates.

The good news is that Makayla was safe. Praise the Lord, Susan and Makayla were already in the service station paying for the diesel fuel. According to the state police and ambulance EMTs, the extinguisher chemicals cause a lack of oxygen that would have been very dangerous for a two-year-old.

The Good News is that we were able to sing on the next night, seven people came to Christ. The pastor emailed us to say that a teenage girl is being baptized before you even read this. A young man in his mid-twenties talked to me that night following the concert and shared how our music and message stirred him to make the decision to accept the Lord. He took rosary beads and a cross from around his neck and told me that his grandmother had given them to him for protection. He handed them to me and said, "All I need is Christ, and I know Him now." As I tucked them into my pocket, I thought—this is what our life is all about. Life on earth doesn't get any better than this.

The good news far outweighs the bad! Like you, we have so much to be thankful for during this season. Have a wonderful Thanksgiving and remember to always have *Joy for the Journey.*

• REUNITED •

While sitting in his van, I listened to a man share an incredible story of love, forgiveness, and anticipation. When I asked if I might write his story for you, he replied, "Sure!"

Over twenty years ago he met a woman, fell in love, and was engaged to be married. One month before the wedding, his wife-to-be told him she had something to tell him. She confessed that she had gotten pregnant as a teen, had a baby boy, and had given him up for adoption. With tears in her eyes, she asked, "Do you still want to marry me?" He replied, "I've already rented the tux and, yes, I want to marry you."

Through the years, this couple had their own family. Although no one else knew about her past, his wife dreamed that one day she would be reunited with the son she had given up for adoption. She wondered if he could ever forgive her even though she acted unselfishly on his behalf. She wondered about his health, schooling and prayed that his parents were giving him the love that he deserved.

A few weeks ago, one of her children got engaged to be married. The house was full of excitement and people were posting congratulations on their Facebook wall. As she read some of the postings, she gasped and she turned the screen for her husband to read. The message read, "My name is … and if you are who I think you are, you know who I am." There was no doubt in her mind that this was her son. He included a picture of himself which looked exactly like her brother.

The next few days were filled with phone calls and explanations to a son and daughter who hadn't known they had a brother. The husband told me, "I've another son." Although the young man's not his biological son, emotionally and in every other way, he is accepting him as his own.

The little baby boy who was given up for adoption is now in his late twenties. His adoptive parents have both passed away. He had never been told of his adoption until his mother was dying.

This Christmas, a family is celebrating a gift that a mother had prayed about for many years. A family has been given a son, a brother, and a loved one. The young man has received an entire family. He thought he had no one left in the world, but by reaching out, he has a new family that loves him. In one of their calls, the family discovered he had recently accepted the Lord. How great is that!

I couldn't help but think of the greatest gift that we've ever received. On the very first Christmas, God gave us his son, Jesus Christ. If you've reached out to receive Him as your Savior, you've been adopted into the family of God.

Have a Blessed Christmas and like this family, may you have *Joy for the Journey.*

• Saving Prayer •

If I had a nickel for every time someone came to me before or after a concert and said, "I've been praying for my loved one for years," I'd be rich. I always respond by telling people not to give up and encourage them to keep on praying. Then I tell them a story about how God has answered prayer.

Recently a couple came to our product table following the concert and asked me if I remembered a couple who had been sitting with them at another concert of ours several weeks before. With all the people we meet, I confessed that I couldn't remember them and could not picture them at all.

The husband told me that he had served with the other man in the Korean Conflict back in the '50s. Since their Army days, they have stayed in contact and the two couples get together two or three times each year.

Throughout the years, the couple talking with me told me that they had witnessed to and prayed for his old Army buddy and his wife. For over fifty-five years, they have prayed for that couple's salvation.

Two years ago we were singing in a city near their friends, so they encouraged them to attend our concert. Following the concert, the unsaved couple related to them that after hearing our son, Richard, share about the miraculous healing of his daughter, they believed there was a God.

This was a huge acknowledgment by a couple who were not saved and had been unwilling to recognize that there was a God. The couple talking to me said that conversation spurred them on to pray for their friends even harder.

Two months ago we returned for another concert in the city near where their friends lived, and the couple came back to hear us.

A few days after the concert, the unsaved friends drove to visit the couple who were talking with me. Their first words blurted out were, "Praise the Lord, we got saved!" Fifty-five years of praying for their salvation had been answered.

Words cannot express how happy both couples were. I believe there was great rejoicing in Heaven as well.

What an encouragement this story was to our family as they encouraged us to keep doing what God has called us to do. They stood before me to say, "Thank you," but the real thanks go to the praying couple and, more importantly, to a Savior who loved us enough that He died for us as atonement for all our sins. If you have an unsaved son, daughter, husband, wife, mom, dad, loved one—keep praying—God is faithful.

Friends, I am rich! I am not talking about those nickels and material riches; I'm saying that I am rich spiritually. As we begin a new year, I trust that you, too, are saved and rich in Jesus Christ.

Have a Happy New Year and remember that salvation in Jesus Christ gives us true *Joy for the Journey*.

• Known by Love •

Some people want to see the worst in others. They are critical, fault-finding, and can be just plain rude. When I look at others, I try to see their best because everyone has worth and everyone can make contributions to the world in which we live—and I know I'm far from perfect too.

An old chorus tells us, "They will know we are Christians by our love." I often wonder as the world hears our words and sees our actions if they see our love and can tell that we are Christians.

Recently a diesel mechanic told me a man had called him on the phone and done something he had never experienced in all of his years at the garage. What he saw was Christian love in action.

Our motor home had lost so much of its power that we could barely drive up hills. We were moving along at a crawl and desperately in need of repair. As we finally got to the church where we were going to sing, I told my family we would need to find a place to get the motor home repaired the next morning.

We sang that Sunday night and were saying our goodbyes when someone asked how far we were going to be traveling. I told them where we were singing next but that we needed to stop on our way to get the motor home fixed. There was absolutely no doubt as to the work needed or the repairs that would need to be done. In fact, I brushed over the details very quickly.

The next morning we were at the garage waiting for it to open. The repairs took all day and when we were told the work was completed, I went to the desk to pay the bill. The diesel mechanic told me there would be no charge. I told him I didn't understand but thanked him. He said, "If you want to thank someone—thank the man who called me on the phone and said he'd take care of the whole bill." The mechanic said he'd never had anyone do this before. He was just blown away by a man who had been at the church the night before and found out where we had gone. Perhaps for the first time in his life, the mechanic was tender-hearted toward the Gospel of Jesus Christ. He said that he'd been yelled at, sworn at, and even blamed for mechanical problems, but that day he'd seen Christian love in action.

To be honest, we were blown away, too. That's real love. There are a lot of good Christian people in this world.

This Valentine's Day, let's show love to our sweethearts and to others less-deserving so the world will see that we are Christians. Let's also express our love to the Lord, who loved us enough to die for us.

I will always try to see the best in others—that certainly gives me *Joy for the Journey.*

· PROTECTED ·

One Saturday we received a call from the pastor of a church where we had just sung to tell us their two air conditioners had been stolen. The units sat just yards from where we had parked our motorhome beside the church. Thieves had come and taken them. Apparently many have been stolen in the area because they can be stripped down and the copper sold for seventy-five dollars each.

I couldn't help but think about God's protection over us. What if they had come while we were there? What if they had come when the motorhome and trailer were parked while we had gone out to eat?

The church estimated repairing the damage and replacing the air conditioning units will cost about twenty thousand dollars. I'm grieved for their loss, but I'm glad no one was hurt or injured.

My mind raced back to the day we pulled into another church. After we had parked, our eyes were drawn to little circles drawn on the pavement. Then we saw a chalk outline of a large figure.

The pastor explained a policeman had been shot by a woman attempting to break into a car. The small circles were drawn around the bullet casings while the larger drawing was where the policeman fell after he had been shot.

What an eerie feeling to see the crime scene just a few feet in front of where we were parked. We were glad that that police officer was going to recover from his wounds but even happier that we were not caught in the crossfire.

Last year we pulled into a church parking lot and slept. The next morning when we went into the church to set up our equipment, the pastor asked if we'd heard anything during the night. Apparently burglars had come that night and broken into the church storage shed while we were sleeping. We hadn't heard a thing!

I'm sure glad the Bible tells us that God never slumbers or sleeps. He is always watching over us. All three of these bad things have happened just before, during, or after we have sung.

If you are reading this and thinking—*those people have lots of bad luck*—I've got news for you. First, I don't believe in luck. God is always in control and He orders our days. Second, my point in sharing these stories is to share how God has faithfully protected us. Many times as we go through our days, we miss the goodness of God. Psalm 46:10-11 says, *be still and know that I am God… The Lord of hosts is with us.* These three incidents would be almost humorous if they weren't so serious and could have had such a negative effect on us.

Sometimes our travels are a delight and sometimes they are difficult, but we always try to see God's hand upon us. As each of us journey through this life, we need to lean on the Lord and have *Joy for the Journey.*

• Apple Tree •

Shortly before he went to be with the Lord, our family had the privilege of singing at an event with Jim Hamill (formerly of the Kingsmen).

After we had finished our set, we stood off-stage and listened as Jim sang and told the famous "Apple Tree" story as he had done many times before. This wonderful story is about a rebellious young man who left home and for two years wandered around the country. Then he accepted Jesus Christ as his Savior. The young man got on a train to head home and found himself seated next to a preacher. He shared that he had written home and told his parents to tie a white rag on their apple tree if he was welcome to come home.

Tears rolled down my cheeks that day as Jim masterfully told how the prodigal son returned home. His parents greeted him standing beside the railroad tracks holding a welcome home sign in front of the apple tree covered with white rags.

I leaned over to Susan and said, "One day I'd like to do that story in our concerts." Years ago, we recorded the "Apple Tree" story and have used the powerful message in many concerts.

A couple of weeks ago I told that story once again. Following the concert an older couple came up to me, told me that the story had ministered to them and that they had a story to tell me.

Their son had left home twenty-one years ago. Both husband and wife said their hearts were broken and they longed to know where he was and if he was dead or alive.

On their 50th wedding anniversary, their son called his sister to ask if she thought their Mom and Dad would mind if he called them. Of course she told him to call them, so after twenty-one years he finally called his parents. They welcomed his call with love and forgiveness. After all these years, they were reunited and he has called them every day since.

They were obviously humbled and broken as they shared with me the joy of receiving their prodigal son back into their lives.

Receiving a son or daughter back after all those years would take a lot of grace and love. Many people would want to yell and scold the prodigal, but to welcome them back with open arms is incredible!

Because this couple had a Christ-like attitude, they were able to restore their joy and repair a broken home and relationship.

We never know when we sing a song how the words will affect the listener. Sometimes they laugh and sometimes they cry, but we always want to be relevant and make a difference spiritually in people's lives.

I can honestly say the couple that told us their story was filled to overflowing with the joy of the Lord. As each of us seeks to be more Christ-like in our love and forgiveness, we will also know *Joy for the Journey.*

• Running the Race •

On a day off while we were in Florida this winter, we decided to go to a theme park. I'll not mention its name, but it is the only place where Susan will go where there is a mouse. She screams at the sight of them anywhere else. Everywhere at the park people were running and racing from ride to ride and pushing their way to get ahead at the attractions.

As we were going to another ride, we noticed a young person walking by wearing a T-shirt with the slogan: *Running the Race, Hebrews 12:1.*

This verse says, *let us run with endurance the race that is set before us.* That sure puts things into perspective. Everyone seems to be so busily racing around when the only race that counts is the one we race for Jesus Christ.

Recently someone found out that our family sings about two hundred fifty dates each year and travels fifty-two weeks each year. He looked at us and said, "Why would you ever do that? Do you have gypsy blood in you?" I must confess that his questions took me by surprise.

I don't have gypsy blood in me, but I have been saved by the blood of Jesus Christ. We race and travel around the United States and Canada to share the good news of Christ and a message of encouragement to believers because we believe it is what God has called us to do.

Last week we received a telephone call from a man who had just gotten home from our cruise. He asked how he could get us to come to his church. We told him we would have to travel a long way, but we could do come. He said he'd pay us himself if the church couldn't or wouldn't. (I'd sure like to have two hundred fifty more of him each year). A week later the pastor emailed us to confirm the date.

When we called the pastor to talk about all of the arrangements he said, "That man's wife accepted Christ when she was on the cruise with you." Apparently while I was preaching at a chapel and our family sang, she made the life-changing decision to repent of her sins and receive Christ. That explained the man's excitement and urgency to get us there this summer.

Is running the race for Jesus Christ worthwhile? Is racing from city-to-city and state-to-state worthwhile? My answer—"Yes!" An old hymn says, "it will be worth it all when we see Christ." Many people seem busy, but we need to be busy doing the business of the Lord.

To the man who boldly wore his T-shirt at the theme park—I applaud you. To the man who recently saw his wife come to Christ—I rejoice with you. To those of you who are running the race with endurance toward the goal that is set before us—experience *Joy for the Journey* and keep running that race 'til Jesus comes.

• Turn Here •

Almost all men hate to ask for driving directions. Some men will drive in circles for hours or go many extra miles before they will stop and ask someone for help.

I thought I'd solved that problem a few years ago when I purchased a GPS device. For those of you who don't use them or know what they are, let me just say that they are an electronic gizmo that gives driving directions. You type in the address where you want to go and the GPS provides you turn-by-turn directions.

We call ours Mrs. Garmin because while we are driving, a woman's voice can be heard giving us directions. Usually, she's pretty good, but sometimes we are disheartened when she says "recalculating" or even "impossible."

Recently while going through Virginia late at night, one of us was driving and the rest of us were sound asleep. At least I was asleep until I felt us slowing down and taking an exit. I reasoned in my mind that we were probably stopping for diesel. I dozed back off until I heard wooden slats under our tires. Mrs. Garmin was taking us on a shortcut and we were crossing a wooden bridge out in the countryside. I jumped out of bed and said, "Let's recalculate back onto the highway."

Shortly after that, we were on the Capital Beltway going around Washington, D.C. As we were crossing the Potomac River on a bridge that has been there for years, Mrs. Garmin began to squawk and tell us to turn left. We were right in the middle of the bridge and would have plunged into the river had we listened to her.

How could she take us over a wooden bridge that isn't even on my map and not recognize this big bridge that has been in place for years? I don't have an answer to that question, but I can tell you that we all laughed about her oddities. It's too bad Mrs. Garmin is not real and cannot know how much fun and joy she gave us on that bridge as we all looked over the side and knew she was leading us overboard.

I still don't want to stop and ask for directions. I guess it's a man thing. So while we are on the road, we rely on maps and the GPS. For the most part, that little electronic device gets me where I need to go.

I know that the only directions and instructions for life that are reliable are found in the Word of God. The Bible is true and can be trusted. The Bible always gives the right way of living life and the perfect directions to eternal life.

I'm very happy to not have to stop and ask directions on my earthly journey, but following the Bible and the voice of God brings me great joy on the journey to eternal life. Follow God's Word for your life's directions and have *Joy for the Journey.*

• Expecting the Unexpected •

W hen least expected, the unexpected is bound to happen.

We had set up all of our equipment in a high school auditorium and the crowds had been seated for the concert. As we began to sing our first song, a thunderstorm blew up suddenly. *Crash!* A thunderbolt of lightning struck and we were plunged into darkness. All that could be heard was a gasp as everything went dark and silent.

After reassuring the crowd, we ran outside in the rain and strung a cord from our motorhome generator to the sound system. Everything worked perfectly except that we were thoroughly soaked. Fortunately, the audience couldn't see us very well in the semi-dark auditorium until the very last song when all the lights came back on. I don't know if the people were clapping and cheering for us or that the power was restored, but I hope the applause was for us and the message of restoration they'd heard.

One of our biggest logistical challenges is when there are potted plants on the stage/platform. Our fear is that one of us will kick them over or get a microphone cord tangled up in a plant. At one church, around Easter, there were lots of lilies and tulips on the platform. My wife began to sneeze as soon as we began setting up. These special plants had been placed in memory of loved ones, so we couldn't very well move them even though Susan is allergic to them. Near the end of the concert, my worst nightmare became a reality. I jumped off the stage to get closer to the people and my cord got caught on a plant. The more I moved and sang, the more I knew something was wrong because the audience was becoming very wide-eyed. Yes, they were watching that plant teeter on the edge of the platform, fall off, and crash to the floor. What a mess! I was very embarrassed, to say the least.

Another unexpected problem happened last week when we sang in a church that had very few electrical outlets up front. We plugged our sound system into an outlet on the floor just a few feet behind where we would be standing to sing.

During the concert, my son stepped back during a song and *Bang!* He had stepped on the cord, broken the connection, and caused the system to quit. We hurriedly found another cord, plugged it in, and kept going.

These events happened when we least expected them. I believe that is exactly what will happen very soon in this world. When we least expect it, the trumpet will sound and the King of Kings and Lord of Lords will return. Friends, the King is coming and if you know Jesus, you will be taken up to meet Him in the air.

We are not supposed to predict the future, but I think we should watch expectantly for His coming, be prepared for the rapture, and have *Joy for the Journey.*

· Angels to the Rescue ·

One May, we were invited to Canada to perform six concerts. Preparing to cross the border is always a challenge. With passports in hand, a detailed list of all our sound equipment, and an inventory of our CDs and DVDs and other products, we approached the customs offices.

We'd heard that some groups were only required to pay thirteen percent duty on their product while others have been asked to unload and explain everything on their bus. Some groups have told us that getting through the border has taken more than six hours.

That being said, you can imagine we approached the crossing with a little fear and trepidation. We said a quick prayer as we got close and were relieved that the customs officer was so nice. She asked a few questions, took care of the business quickly, and told us to have a great week.

God had answered our prayers and we felt as if an angel had been sent to help us. Could she have been an angel? She might have been, but we'll never know on this side of heaven.

A friend of ours who was helping us drive wanted a cup of coffee, so three of us walked into *Tim Horton's*. We hadn't exchanged any money and didn't have any Canadian dollars. The total came up on the cash register and I gave the cashier US funds to cover the cost. She looked at me and said, "I need more to cover the exchange rate." I replied, "How much more do you need?" She said, "I don't know, but if you keep giving me money I'll tell you when it's enough." The cash register was programmed to do the exchange.

I kept giving her money and she kept pushing the button until she said I'd given her enough. Our driver/friend just laughed and laughed and said, "I don't know who is crazier—the cashier for not know the exchange rate or you for continuing to hand her money." I think I was the crazy one for giving her money until she said she had enough.

We found that the people in Nova Scotia and New Brunswick were very friendly and thought the country was extremely beautiful. We laughed at ourselves for not knowing the exchange rates. We constantly tried to figure out how fast we could drive at fifty kilometers per hour. It also boggled our minds trying to figure out how far we had to drive if we had one hundred kilometers to go and what the temperature was at thirty degrees Celsius. Can anyone tell me how many liters equal a gallon and the cost of a gallon of diesel when it's priced in Canadian dollars per liter?

The best part of the trip was that eight people trusted Christ as their Savior during our concerts.

Friends, learn to laugh at yourselves and know that God is in control. We've got a great big wonderful God who always gives *Joy for the Journey*!

· Kids Are Great! ·

While getting ready for kindergarten, a little boy told his grandmother that he had an appointment with his teacher for testing and screaming. His grandmother said, "I think it's screening," to which he replied, "Oh no, it's screaming."

Aren't kids great? We love to see them at our concerts. We're happy that so many young people still love and enjoy gospel music.

A few years ago we met a little boy at a church where we were singing. He was with his mom and stepfather. During the conversation, we learned that the boy's biological father was in prison. I couldn't imagine the pain he must have felt and the emotional roller-coaster he was on.

We meet a lot of people every week, but this little boy really made an impact on us. We prayed that we also made an impact on his life. Through the years, we have seen him off and on and knew he had a really tough life.

A few months ago someone told us that the boy's father had been released from prison. They said he had turned his life around and had won total custody of his son. Apparently the boy's mother and stepfather divorced and she was not living a very good life.

In July, we sang at a Bible Conference that also has a children's camp on the grounds. What a great surprise to once again meet that same boy who is now a teenager. He is working at the camp doing dishes and maintenance. His dad told him he could have a free week at basketball camp if he worked at the Bible camp all summer.

He is attending two chapels each day, studying his Bible, memorizing verses, learning more about God, and working hard. Not only did this boy's father change his own life around, he is working hard to raise his son to know and love God also.

We are so glad that our journey has allowed our paths to cross so many times with this boy. He will never know how often we have thought about him and prayed for him. To see this struggling little boy turn into a God-fearing young man is such a joy.

All the other kids at camp have money on account so they can buy things in the Snack-Shack. We found out that this boy didn't have any money. He has worked so hard and the camp director said he never complains.

Before we left, we put a small amount of money on his Snack-shack account. Sure wish we could've seen his face when he realized he could enjoy some snacks.

Kids are great! The investment in their lives will pay eternal dividends.

Sometimes we may see a difference right away, other times it may be years, or perhaps it won't be until heaven when we find out about the impact we've had on others. No matter when, making a difference and reaching out to others will always give *Joy for the Journey.*

· HIS EYE IS ON THE SPARROW ·

We were five hours from home and had another seven hours to drive before we would reach our destination. The concert that night had been planned for quite a while and lots of promotion and advertising had been done.

There was little traffic between five thirty a.m. and six a.m. that morning as I drove down the highway. All of a sudden I looked down at the gauges and saw something wrong. I knew I had to pull off to the side, but that can be dangerous if you can't get off far enough. Looking up quickly I saw a sign, *Truck Rest Area*. We coasted off the highway and came to a stop. God had kept us safe and protected by allowing us to break down by a rest area.

I called a wrecker because it was obvious that we needed to be towed to a diesel repair garage. It took six hours for the wrecker to arrive, hook us up, and tow us to the garage.

Now we had two other problems. First, that night's concert had to be canceled. The second problem was that the wrecker could only take one of us and the other three adults and Makayla couldn't be left at the rest area for the rest of the day. God had already put us in a rest area and He certainly wasn't going to let us down now.

I called the promoter—his reaction was unbelievable! He understood and asked about our next available date. I told him we were booked the next day, but we could come in forty-eight hours if that would work for him. He booked us and said, "Someone will be there that needs your concert." Wow—God is so good.

Now, what was I going to do with my family? I thought about a rental car and then aha! Our ministry has an accountant to keep our books and do our taxes. I've only met him a few times, but we talk on the phone frequently. I remembered that he lived in that area, so I picked up my cell phone and called. He answered, said he only lived ten minutes from where we were, that his wife could come pick up my family, and they could stay at his home until everything was fixed. By six p.m., the repairs were complete and we were back on the road again.

I don't pretend to understand why we broke down, but I could certainly see the hand of God everywhere I turned.

Forty-eight hours later, we started singing at our re-scheduled concert. The attendance was double that of the previous year and we could just sense the spirit of God.

When we finished, one lady told my wife, "You are here just for me tonight!" Later another person told me and my son, "You were here just for me." The promoter was right.

How can you see the hand of God at work and not have *Joy for the Journey?*

• Perfect Timing •

There are so many times when I'm going through something or praying about something that I think, *I wish God would hurry up!* or *Why is He so slow?*

I've sung the chorus, "In His Time," all my life. Our family has frequently sung a song titled, "He's Never Been Too Late." Yet, often times I am impatient and think God should be on my time schedule.

In September, we were making our annual journey to the National Quartet Convention in Louisville, Kentucky. On the way, we had scheduled concerts in Pennsylvania and Ohio.

Wednesday was supposed to be a travel day and we needed to be in Pennsylvania on Thursday evening. I had calculated the miles and knew exactly how far we needed to drive before we could pull over and get some sleep on Wednesday night.

The problem was that nothing seemed to go right all day long. First, we had a very small problem with our coach, so I called ahead and asked a service center if they could help me. They told me to stop and they would have me out in half an hour. We stopped for the quick fix. Four hours later we were still delayed and being repaired. I began to pace and mumble and must have asked the service manager a dozen times how things were going. Some of you probably do exactly what I did and others of you think *he needs more patience.* Now I'm not going to pray for more patience because I know the Bible says that trials work patience.

I certainly don't think I need any more trials!

We ended up leaving six hours later than I had planned with all of my figuring and wisdom.

It wasn't long before it got dark and it was raining so hard it was difficult to see. The wipers didn't seem to go fast enough to keep the windshield clean so I made the decision to pull over and sleep a while. The next morning I got up and started to drive again. It was still raining, but at least it was light.

As we got on the NY Thruway heading west, I noticed a big sign with the message that several exits were closed due to flooding. I got within two miles of the exit that we needed to take to go into Pennsylvania and my cell phone rang. The frantic voice on the other end of the line said, "We've got to cancel tonight. We are getting the remnants of tropical storm Lee and we are under water. We are in a State of Emergency and even if you got in, you'd never get back out of here."

If we had arrived there on my time schedule, we would have been in trouble. God's timing is perfect and He protected us even if it meant being held up at the service center.

Happy Thanksgiving and remember, when we trust God's perfect timing, there is *Joy for the Journey.*

· CHRISTMAS WISHES ·

I t's beginning to look a lot like Christmas everywhere I go." The sights and sounds of the Christmas season are all around us. Christmas music is filling the air at grocery stores, malls, restaurants, and best of all, in church.

Today I found myself singing, "it's the most wonderful time of the year." We will be singing Christmas Eve, but plan to get home by two a.m. on Christmas morning. After a little sleep, we will spend time as a family reading Luke 2 before exchanging gifts and sitting down to a big meal.

God gave us the greatest gift—His Son, Jesus. Since His birth, the tradition has been to exchange gifts with loved ones and friends.

I am always amazed at how much people spend for presents and I'm even more shocked to hear how people take all year long to pay off their Christmas debts. I fear that we have lost the real meaning of Christmas and the reason for the season.

I've been asking some children and adults what they want for Christmas this year. It's interesting how long the lists are and there is no doubt in my mind that we are a *gimme* generation.

Then recently, I was told by three different people what they wanted for Christmas and their wishes gave me hope for mankind.

I was rolling cords up after our concert when a lady approached me and said, "You gave me hope and encouragement tonight. We found out today that my fifteen-year-old grandson has a brain tumor and needs to see the oncologist on Monday. All I want for Christmas is for God to heal my grandson." She doesn't want anything for herself; she only cares about her grandchild.

A man had tears in his eyes last night when he told me that his son is serving in Iraq. He told me that he was expecting him home for Christmas. In fact, all he wanted for Christmas was to hold his son in his arms and know that he was safely home.

Last week I was standing behind our product table selling CDs when a girl in her late twenties stepped up in line. What she told me caused me to stop everything I was doing and pay attention to her. She told me she was pregnant and had just found out she had cervical cancer. She went on to say that doctors planned to take the baby at thirty-two weeks and then take care of her. All she wants this Christmas is to know she will live to raise this baby.

All of our wish lists pale and seem so insignificant in comparison to these requests and prayers. And all the gifts we can give each other pale and seem so insignificant in comparison to the gift God gave us—His Son, Jesus! During this Christmas season, let me encourage you and remind myself that we've received the greatest Gift of all, enabling us to have *Joy for the Journey*.

· A New Beginning ·

How exciting it is to be entering a brand new year! Sometimes we wish we could know what is ahead for our lives, families, ministries, and country. I'm so glad God is in control and that He is the one who knows our tomorrows and not us.

One October, we were taken by surprise several times. We found new meaning in the phrase, "it's a hit." We backed into a dumpster, then we hit a deer, and after that, a big bird—all in one weekend! I'd like to say that they all three jumped out in front of us, but you know better.

If I had known that we were going to hit these things, I would have acted and reacted differently. I'm sure glad I didn't know what was ahead. I'm also thankful that God protected us from harm.

Later that same month, we were in the dressing room getting ready for a concert. My son was changing his pants and was standing in his boxer shorts when the door opened. A man and two ladies burst through the door and said, "We've heard you on the radio, but we've never seen you in person." There was no place to hide and we didn't exactly want to be seen that way.

We've laughed about that incident many times since, but we weren't amused at the time even though they didn't even seem to care or notice. Now you know why I don't think knowing what's ahead is the best for us.

Even though I may not know what will come my way next year,

I do know we are one step closer to the coming of the Lord. Certainly it can't be long until the trumpet sounds and we will go to be with Him.

The last week of October, my wife and I were going through a check-out counter at a store in Delaware. The young man running the cash register, who was probably in his early twenties, said, "Can you believe it's going to snow so early this year?" He went on to say that it was scary that we've seen so many tornadoes and had so much flooding in our country this year. He opened the door so I couldn't resist talking about the earthquakes, tsunamis, wars, and rumors of wars that we've heard about these last few months.

Not that I'm predicting that Jesus will come this year because the Bible tells us not to set dates, but I do think we ought to be living as if He might come at any moment.

Whatever comes our way this year, I encourage us all to keep our eyes on the Lord, to allow Him to guide us, and to walk with Him. Whether we go through the best of times or difficult trials, if our relationship with God is what it should be, we can always sing and say, "It is well with my soul" and have *Joy for the Journey*. Happy New Year!

• LOVE IS IN THE AIR •

They say, "love is in the air," but sometimes I have a hard time finding love in the world.

We returned home after a recent tour to find our furnace had stopped working so I called a repairman to come look at it. Someone forgot to tell the dispatcher, who happened to be a woman, about this thing called love. She was extremely rude and basically told me the service technician would get here when he gets here. There was anything but love in the air with that conversation. As you read this story, just picture me dressed in a jacket, hat, and mittens as I write and wait for the man to come and fix the furnace. The only thing I feel in the air at my house is a chill.

I planned to write about love, but I just went out to the mailbox. A letter from the bank announced that a check that we had been given bounced and, in fact, was written on a closed account. We paid a five dollar fee to sing at that event. I guess they didn't really intend to give us anything—their love wasn't too great. They stole from me, but I can't let them rob me of my joy and love.

February 14th is a great day to express love and I'm so glad that I have some people in my life that show me love and allow me to love them back.

Over thirty-five years ago, my wife, Susan, and I stood before God and our friends and said, "I do." Our marriage has been a love story. She has faithfully stood beside me in life and on the stage. Life on the road is not always easy, but she climbs in our coach week after week. She is always encouraging me spiritually and never hesitates to tell me that she loves me.

I thank the Lord every day that He sent her into my life and also for these many years that have gone by so quickly. I love her today as much or more as the day I said, "I do." Love is still in the air.

Some red roses or a box of chocolates seem so insignificant compared to the significance that my Susan gives to me. She deserves the world, not just a mere token.

My most constant friend, who loves me unconditionally, is the Lord. He died for me, rose again, lives for me, and is coming back for me. What love!

The reason I can have joy for the journey is found in one word and one name—Jesus.

The world is not always a kind and loving place, but all of us have people in our lives that bring us love, joy, and happiness. Be sure to express your love during this "Love Month" and don't forget the Lord. As you tell the Lord and the special people in your lives that you love them, you'll find *Joy for the Journey*.

· A GLAMOROUS LIFE? ·

Many people think gospel singers live a glamorous life. I don't know how many times people have said to me, "It must be wonderful to travel and see the country." I've stopped telling them we often drive all night and you can't see that much in the dark. I've also stopped telling them that six of us living in our coach gets crowded and that we have no privacy.

Recently our glamorous life found us on the side of the road with a blown inside rear tire. When the tire blew, it ripped the air hose which takes care of the airbags and brakes. All this happened around five p.m. one night and was finally repaired and ready to go by ten a.m. the next morning. The repair bill was high, but at least we made the concert that night.

With five days off this week, I found myself in the repair garage again for maintenance on the coach. Although it was supposedly a one-day repair, three days later I was still waiting. I had arrived on Monday night for a first thing Tuesday morning appointment. At six forty-five a.m., I was at the door with people starting to line up behind me for the seven a.m. opening.

Can you imagine people being that anxious to get to church or to a gospel concert?

A few years ago, my son and his wife had their second child. My grandson was born when we were singing fifteen hundred miles away from home. Richard has sung with us for fifteen years and loves every minute, but missing your child's birth and not being able to be with your wife during that wonderful moment is not wonderful.

You may think I sound negative or bitter, but there couldn't be anything further from the truth. Singing gospel music and traveling from city to city is not as glamorous as one might think, but does bring us joy.

There is joy in knowing you are doing what God has called you to do. There is no greater joy than leading someone to Jesus Christ. There is joy in hugging and helping hurting people, in reaching out to someone who has lost a loved one, in talking to a pastor who is so discouraged he is ready to quit, or in taking the time to stop and listen to someone who has just been diagnosed with cancer. The list goes on and on, but all of those examples are exactly things we have done this month. If our life is glamorous, let me suggest that *every* Christian is living a glamorous life if he or she is truly living for the Lord.

We all have the privilege and responsibility to reach out to a lost world and reach in to our brothers and sisters in Christ. No matter what job we may be called to do, we need to do our work to the glory of God and then we will have *Joy for the Journey.*

· Nothing Surprises God ·

As we were waiting to be introduced at a concert in January, the emcee said, "We've got an announcement. One of our young couples has to air flight their two-week-old son to a larger hospital because he is having heart problems." Where there had been excitement in the crowd, there were now gasps of silence as if all the air had been sucked out of the room.

Almost immediately, the emcee continued, "Now let's welcome the Hyssongs." I thought, *what are we going to do?* We stepped out and sang "I'm Expecting a Miracle" and then stopped everything and led the people in prayer before singing "God Still Can."

Ministering to that group of people and not worrying about our program or plan was important. We needed to be sensitive to their needs and be willing to be used of God.

When I said, "Let's pray for this family," the whole place was in one accord. They wanted to bow before Almighty God to ask Him to heal this baby boy and to be with the parents.

After we had prayed, the audience was ready for us to sing. The announcement may have taken us all by surprise, but nothing surprises God.

Later we learned that the mother of this infant was the daughter of South American missionaries. Her father had been taken hostage when she was a little girl, held for a couple of years, and then killed.

She has seen so much hurt in her life. No wonder the people in the audience were so upset. They had financially supported the family on the field, helped them through the death of a loved one, and been a part of this woman's wedding and pregnancy. Now she might lose her child.

We had a choice that night to ignore what was happening or change our concert and minister to the people. To ignore the situation would have spelled disaster. Right then they didn't need to hear a song or a joke; they needed to hear from God.

How can the daughter of a slain missionary go on? How can the mother of this two-week-old infant keep trusting God and have an unwavering faith? How can she know joy?

The answer is simple. We have a risen Savior, who loved us enough to die for us, be buried, and then rise again three days later. Easter is not about the eggs, candy, or bunnies. Easter is about our reason for life and hope.

We cannot know why trials and tribulations come into our lives, but I know the One, who can help us in our time of sickness, hurt, and loss. His name is Jesus.

Let's reach out to people around us who need help, hope, and encouragement. Easter is the one special day of the year that we celebrate the resurrection of Jesus Christ. For the Christian, Easter is a reminder that we have a living Savior and that knowledge is enough to give us *Joy for the Journey.*

· LIFE SAVERS ·

Recently I've been thinking about three men who walked the aisle one Sunday to accept Christ. Their actions etched a lasting memory in my mind. Last month another man, whom we had the privilege to lead to Christ about ten years ago, told us he was going to retire early and go into missions' work. I'll never forget the day of his salvation or his announcement that many others will now be able to hear the Gospel.

On January 23, 2012, our son, Richard, and his wife had their second child. The baby is a boy, so now we have a granddaughter and a grandson. We are taking lots of pictures and making memories.

Another unforgettable memory occurred last summer when Richard called to tell me a skunk had gotten into his garage. He said, "Should I shut the door?" Of course, I told him to leave the door up and the animal would eventually leave. The skunk did leave but left his scent behind as a reminder of his visit. How could I ever forget that day or the many times we've laughed about it?

May is a great month to honor people and events. Stopping to remember is a wonderful activity!

First, we ought to remember our mothers on Mothers' Day. Our mothers risked their lives to bring us into this world. Most of them sacrificed and went without so we could have the shoes, clothes, and even toys they provided for us.

My mom took me to church and always had Life Savers to keep me quiet. I'll always remember her cooking, cleaning, and taking time for me. She never got upset and didn't say a word when I went fishing, brought home the fish we'd caught, and let them swim in our bathtub. I even used my bed for a trampoline and kept touching the white ceiling with my dirty hands. She stopped me only after my sister tattled.

Most of us are where we are today because our mothers prayed for us. We wish a Happy Mothers' Day to all the moms reading this article. To my mom, ninety years young, "Thanks, Mom, I love you."

May is also a month to remember those who went off to war and never returned. Without the sacrifices of sons, daughters, fathers, and mothers, we would not enjoy the freedoms that we enjoy today. Memorial Day is not just a day for picnics and fireworks; it is a day to remember those who gave their lives to keep us free as well as those who mourn their loss. Let's never forget! May we always fly our flags high, thankfully sing "The Star Spangled Banner," and stand proud to be Americans.

Remembering the sacrifices made on our behalf is good. But I never want to forget a Savior who sacrificed His life for me that I might live, who rose from the dead, and who is coming again. Christ is the One, who truly brings *Joy for the Journey.*

· Mistaken Identity ·

Mistaken identity and misunderstandings can certainly cause problems. The other day I was twentieth in line to mail some posters at the post office. We shuffled ahead at a tediously slow pace until I finally reached the front of the line. The clerk had just begun to help me when suddenly an older lady walked up, pointed her finger at me, and yelled! She accused me of parking in a handicapped spot and told me how I could be fined or towed away. As she screamed at me in front of other customers, I must have turned several shades of red, but I just held my tongue.

The clerk looked at me with inquisitive eyes so I said, "I don't even know where the handicapped parking is located." He asked me where I was parked and I pointed to my car. The clerk said, "You aren't parked in a handicapped spot." He smiled at me saying, "She must have thought you were someone else and mistook you for driving another car." He understood, but I have to wonder about the fifteen to twenty people in line who heard her tirade.

I have to confess, I sort of felt sorry for myself until we went to our next concert. The minister of music told us a story about a young woman who had come to his office. She was covered in tattoos and had several body piercings with rings. She asked, "Can I be saved?" He assured her she could if that's what she wanted. She related she had been going to another church where the pastor told her she could not be saved because of the way she looked. Talk about being mistaken. I'm glad the song, "Just as I Am," is true.

He went on to tell her that God loved her and had a plan for her life regardless of how she looked. He then joyfully led her to Christ. The woman has been faithfully coming to church with her husband and little girl every week. She dresses differently and looks different now that she knows she's a child of God.

A couple of weeks ago the woman brought a friend to church. The Music Minister was standing near the nursery when she was dropping off her daughter and heard her talking to her friend. "They dress a little funny here, but once you get to know them, they are very nice." The pastor said he had to chuckle because he had never heard that comment or considered that perspective before.

The lady in the post office mistakenly identified me as someone breaking the law, but she was wrong. The church that mistakenly identified the young lady with the tattoos as someone who couldn't become saved was also wrong. I'm glad that although we are all different in the way we look or dress, God loves each of us.

Realizing God's love for each of us in our uniqueness makes me smile and gives *Joy for the Journey.*

· Hot-Foot Dance ·

When traveling from concert to concert on extended tours, we have a hard time finding two things. The first is a laundromat—we are always on the lookout for them. We do not have a washer/dryer on our coach, but we do have four adults along with two children. I wouldn't trade singing with my family and having the grandchildren along with us for anything, but laundry needs to be done on a regular basis.

The second thing that seems to accumulate is garbage. How can we have so many bags of trash? Every time we stop at a rest area or for fuel, one of us gathers it up and tries to find a dumpster.

Recently we stopped at a popular barbecue restaurant. After we ate a delicious meal, the owner graciously told us we could throw our trash in his dumpster.

My son, Richard, put on his sandals, picked up the bags of garbage and headed out back. The dumpster was quite tall and he is not, so he looked around to see what he could use to stand on to get the lids up. He saw a mound he thought was dirt and decided he could climb on it, lift the lids, and get rid of the bags. As he stepped up on the mound and lifted the lid, he began to sink. The mound wasn't dirt but used hot ashes from the barbecue smoker.

When his sandals began to sink in the hot ashes, I can guarantee you that he moved pretty fast. People often comment about his movements on the stage, but they haven't seen anything until they watched his hot-foot dance.

We all laughed, but I still don't think he sees the humor in the whole incident.

July is a great month for family, barbecues, and gospel music, but my advice is to avoid standing in hot ashes. This is especially true if you are going to wear sandals.

I thought there must be a lesson to learn from all of this. That mound of dirt looked really attractive to Richard, but in actuality hurt him.

We all need to be careful that we don't go where we shouldn't and that we don't do things that are not pleasing to God. When we sink in sin, not only are we hurt but those around us are too.

We not only need to keep our laundry clean, we need to keep our lives clean. We should also keep the trash out of our lives by confessing our sin to the Lord. The Bible tells us, *[Jesus] is faithful and just to forgive us our sins, and to cleanse us from all unrighteousness.* (1 John 1:9)

Enjoy the summer, have fun with your family and friends, and enjoy your relationship with God. As long as I have breath to speak and ink in my pen, I'll keep saying that as we maintain the proper relationship with the Lord, He will give us *Joy for the Journey!*

• WHAT WILL PEOPLE THINK? •

Have you ever gone out to eat and everything went wrong? We recently had that experience, and, needless to say, the occasion was unforgettable.

Once we were seated, a waitress who was being trained came to our table followed by the waitress who was teaching her. She asked what we wanted to drink and everyone ordered water except my young granddaughter who wanted chocolate milk and my Coke.

When she returned with our tray of drinks, she started taking the glasses off until the tray became unbalanced and the chocolate milk went flying through the air covering the table, my wife, and me.

She was just learning and everyone makes mistakes, so we shrugged and asked for more napkins so we could dry ourselves. She finally brought a few napkins but never said she was sorry.

Next I put a straw in my soda and took a sip. It tasted awful! Obviously the fountain drink did not get the appropriate mixture of syrup and seltzer. I wondered if I was imagining things, so everyone at the table took a sip and came to the same conclusion.

When I finally got the waitress's attention, I told her quietly about it and she walked away saying she would check it out. Ten minutes later she walked by again and I asked her a second time. She said, "I haven't had time, do you want lemonade?" I agreed and talked with the family thinking the service and food couldn't get any worse—but it did.

When the food finally came, it was so burnt we couldn't even cut through the meatloaf. She didn't come back during the meal and I think we all can imagine why, even though we were nice to her. The waitress who was supervising her didn't come to check on us either.

We sat there wondering if we should even leave a tip. Finally, we decided we would give a tip, pay the bill, and never return to the restaurant where we have stopped many times before when traveling through that area. Bad service lost them customers.

As I've thought about the dining experience that probably all of us have had at one time or another, I wondered if our churches, radio programs, and concerts have had the same effect.

Do people have a positive experience when they visit our church? When someone tunes into a gospel radio station, what do they think? How do we treat people when they attend a gospel concert? We should want them to have a good experience so they will want to come back or listen again.

I want people to see Jesus in me. I want Him seen in our churches, our gospel radio stations, and in our concerts.

The Bible tells us to be the light and salt of the earth. As we desire to be the light of the world and treat others as we desire to be treated, it is a sure recipe to having *Joy for the Journey.*

· HOLY GROUND ·

Every time someone tells me they have a record we made in the early '70s or a CD of our family that is fifteen years old, I want to buy it back. My appearance has changed and our sound has changed through the years. I suppose every singer is happiest with their newest project. However, following a recent Saturday night concert, a lady approached me to say she had one of our earliest recordings. I cringed and wondered where the conversation would go from there. She went on to say the song "Holy Ground" had made a difference in her life and helped her get through a very difficult time.

She told me that her husband had been diagnosed with colon cancer and she was devastated. He faced surgery and she faced the uncertainty of his recovery and survival. She said she popped our old CD in her player on the way to the hospital and listened as we sang "we are standing on holy ground." She said she listened again and again as we sang about the angels being all around. Those words gave her the strength and courage to sit in the waiting room that day as her husband faced the fight of his life.

As she waited, those powerful words continued to echo in her mind. She thought about the angels surrounding her and her husband. Not only did she think about them, she sensed the presence of the Lord.

I was humbled to think I wanted to take back all those early CDs, but God was using one to help make a difference. She said she was afraid to lose him, but she was even more panicked because he was not saved. She told me she cried out to the Lord and the Great Physician brought her husband through the surgery. On the way home from the hospital that day, she played the song again. She thought *if we are standing on holy ground, why can't my husband come to a saving knowledge of Jesus Christ?*

Once again, she cried out to God to save her husband of thirty years of marriage. Little did she know that one of her best friends planned to visit her husband. A few days after the surgery, the friend visited and asked the husband the question, "Isn't it time you accepted the Lord?" To which he answered, "Yes." Her friend led him to Jesus Christ that day and his life was changed.

Today her husband is not only saved, but he is cancer free. Praise the Lord for a faithful wife who prayed and called upon the Lord for her spouse.

I'm glad that God can use old projects and old songs to reach people and make a difference today. The Lord certainly has a way to make us humble. He can still use the projects I thought were old and not good.

God is in control and that night the lady and I both had *Joy for the Journey.*

· You Can't Fix Stupid ·

A while ago as our family was driving to another concert, we were thinking of several things that had happened in the past few weeks that could have made us mad, but instead made us chuckle.

One Sunday night I had just gotten dressed for the concert. The church was good-sized, but I decided to walk around the building and enter the front door. As I rounded the corner of the building, I could see through three sets of glass doors that a lady was sitting on the floor. I hustled in to ask if she was alright. She said, "Yes, I'm just resting."

Now that seemed odd to me until she explained she had brought her mother to the concert and she just wanted to talk with her. Her mom sat in a wheelchair just inside the doors with her daughter sitting next to her on the floor. Together they watched people enter and they gossiped about each and every person who entered the church. I heard the mother say things such as, "Their son is rebellious," and "That man cheated on his wife." I couldn't believe my ears. A couple came through the door that she didn't recognize so she said, "What church are you from?" When they told her, she said, "That's not a very good church!"

I stood there not knowing whether to laugh or cry and I wondered what she must have said about me when I came in. I thought of an old statement that I've heard many times before, *you can't fix stupid*. Only God can fix and change the heart. Before the concert began that night, I prayed that God would work in her heart and that she would want to be more like Jesus.

A few weeks later we sang at a revival service. When we finished our last song, a well-known speaker got up to deliver the message. When he concluded his message, the altar was filled with people getting right with God. The Spirit of God moved mightily that night. I got up to lead a final song and used one of our microphones. I then passed the mic to the speaker who closed in prayer.

Following the service, the sound man almost ran to the front of the auditorium and complained to my son, "You wrecked the last fifteen minutes of the service!" We looked at each other bewildered and without a clue. We later realized that he was upset because the final prayer went through our sound system and not the house system.

The sound man was so concerned about his sound system he missed the importance of people's lives being changed. Neither that lady nor the sound man is going to rob me of my joy. They have both forgotten what is really important. People are God's priority.

Don't forget to keep your eyes on the Lord and the things that are really important. Until next time, I trust you will have *Joy for the Journey.*

· A God-cidence? ·

Thanksgiving is a time we give thanks to God. I could never write in one article all the things for which I am thankful. There wouldn't be enough ink to write about my Savior—Jesus. I could talk about family and friends and ministry, but let me share something that happened to us the day after the National Quartet Convention.

During the convention, we had a chance to talk to many friends. One of them spent a little time with us and as we shook hands to say goodbye, we wondered when we'd see him again.

We were surprised two days later when he strolled through the door of the church in North Carolina where we were singing. Although we were glad to see him, he obviously did not feel well. We had no more said hello then he sat down and put his hand on his chest. The color of his face turned yellowish-gray—he was in some distress. He decided to go sit in his car to see if he felt better.

I walked to the car with him where he decided he needed to go home. We were disappointed that he felt so ill he had to leave, but stood on the steps of the church feeling concern and nervously watched our sick friend drive away.

Before, during, and after the concert, our family prayed for him and wished we had his cell phone number so we could check on him.

The concert, packing up, and the meal provided by the church took about four hours. We finally left the church and started to drive through the night.

The interstate highway was about a mile down the road. As we approached the ramp, our hearts sank when we saw our friend's car pulled off into the ditch.

We jumped out and checked the front seat of the car. With hearts pounding, we started to shine lights around the grass along the side of the highway. We were frantically calling out for him when a car pulled off the interstate. A young couple rolled down their window and called our friend's name.

We ran over to their car and the young couple said they had stopped earlier and called an ambulance for our sick friend. Together we called the hospital where he had been taken, but he had already been transferred to another. We then called the larger hospital and they said he'd been admitted to the intensive care unit.

We've talked to his family many times since, and he is doing well. He did not have a heart attack as we first suspected, but instead an attack of gall stones.

I'm thankful for the couple who stopped and called the ambulance. I'm also thankful God had that same couple drive back four hours later and tell us what had happened. I'm thankful that God still hears prayers and heals.

Finally, I'm thankful for all of the friends that give us *Joy for the Journey*. Happy Thanksgiving, everyone!

• LASTING LEGACY •

The Christmas song entitled, "It's the Most Wonderful Time of the Year," expresses how I feel right now. I love the decorations, family gatherings, songs, and the reason for the season. The true meaning of our celebration is the birth of Jesus Christ. God gave us the greatest gift that we could ever receive—a Savior—Christ the Lord.

Christmas is a time for giving and yes, it is more *blessed to give than to receive.*

Recently I was talking with a grandmother who told me a story that once again put a smile on my face and demonstrated a sacrificial love that all of us should find refreshing.

She approached the product table and told me about her fourteen-year-old grandson who has Asperger's syndrome autism. As she told me about her special needs grandson, I could see the love and concern she had for him in her eyes and from the words that she spoke.

She shared how her grandson had worn his parents out, so they asked her if she could care for him for a few days. She gladly took him into her home and for two weeks took care of his every need. Though caregiving was hard work, she enjoyed every minute. While he was with her, she played several of our CDs she had purchased at a previous concert. She was so excited that he had learned most of the words and memorized and recited to her several of my narrations.

When his stay at her home came to an end, he looked at his grandmother and said, "This really is a Christian home." What a wonderful gift she has given him.

Just before she came to our concert, her fourteen-year-old grandson asked if she could get him a set of our CDs. She told me she wanted to purchase six but was a little short on cash. Together we worked out a deal because I wanted her to be able to give him the Christmas gift that he really wanted.

I sure wish I could be in their home on Christmas morning and see his face when he opens her gift.

The greatest gift we've ever received is Jesus. The greatest gift a grandmother can give her grandchildren is Jesus.

She has a desire to leave a legacy behind that has eternal value. As we buy our children and grandchildren toys, bicycles, and every material thing we can afford (and sometimes things we cannot afford), I hope all of us will consider what is really important. An important gift may not be one of our CDs that you give your children or grandchildren, but it could be a Bible or a good Christian book. Perhaps the gift may be taking them to church on Christmas Eve or even reading the Christmas story from Luke 2 as you sit around with the family some evening.

Have a wonderful holiday season! As we keep Christ in Christmas, we are sure to have *Joy for the Journey.*

· MISSING! ·

When I think about the New Year, I think of fresh starts and new beginnings. I confess I'm ready for next year to be ushered in because the last year ended with our family being stranded beside the road surrounded by firemen and police.

Our ordeal began late at night when our driver realized the cars behind us were all flashing their headlights. He turned on the backup camera and shouted, "We've lost the trailer." Our hearts stopped because we feared the trailer might have caused an accident and hurt someone. Immediately the driver shouted, "I think we still have the trailer, but we must be dragging it."

He exited and pulled over. We quickly realized that the reason he couldn't see the trailer through the camera was because of all the heavy smoke. We all jumped out and discovered the smoke was coming from the diesel fuel we had spilled.

Very soon, the dark night was filled with lights from two fire trucks, the fire captain's vehicle, and a police car. One of the trucks even raised a huge spotlight that shone on the back of our coach and allowed them to see how much fuel we had lost. The firemen crawled under the coach to assess the situation and the captain called the EPA to see if they wanted to come out and check the diesel spill.

After an hour had passed, the firemen deemed the situation safe— no fire or explosion would occur—and told us to call a wrecker to get our motorhome towed to the service center. The firemen had found a high-pressure fuel line had broken and they were afraid the engine would catch on fire if we tried to start the vehicle.

At the top of the exit, my daughter-in-law waited at a convenience store with our granddaughter and grandson who were four years and nine months respectively at that time. The clerk at the store blew up balloons and helped to keep the kids entertained.

Five firemen waited with us for the wrecker to arrive. Finally, I got the courage to ask if the fire department was going to bill us. The captain said, "No, we are just doing our job." I breathed a sigh of relief and then asked my second question. "Is the EPA going to fine us?" The captain said, "I called them and told them the situation and they said they were not going to fine you."

The captain proceeded to tell us that he would take our family to a hotel nearby the truck service center where the coach was being towed.

In the middle of a difficult and expensive trip, God brought us joy through the people He sent to us that night. The policeman, firemen, EPA person, store clerk, tow-truck driver, hotel clerk, and truck repairman were all so fantastic they gave us joy for our journey.

Happy New Year! I trust you'll be blessed this coming year and also enjoy *Joy for the Journey.*

· Why Worry? ·

Recently I had to have a colonoscopy. As I entered the hospital, I thought to myself, this certainly isn't a joyful journey!

I soon was reminded that every day with the Lord can be a joy for the journey day.

They took me into the preparation room to get ready for the procedure. The nurse who was putting on my blood pressure cuff and inserting the IV looked down at me and said, "I often watch you on television when I'm getting ready to come to work. I love to hear your family sing." I thanked her and knew God had put her there just for me.

The doctor finally came into the room and told me the anesthesiologist was still on another case and running late. I was already anxious about the procedure as I'd been waiting all day until now—four o'clock in the afternoon. I hoped he wouldn't be too much longer.

Music was playing in the room. The doctor came over to my bed and asked if I liked the music or if I'd rather he found some of my family's music. I didn't even know that he knew I sang.

Before I could even answer, he was searching on his telephone through the Internet. He said, "Do you mind if I listen to "It is Well with My Soul" on YouTube?"

With one nurse to my left and another nurse at my head and the doctor leaning over my right side, we all watched and listened to my family singing the hymn, "It is Well with My Soul."

The words, "when peace like a river attendeth my way," helped me relax and once again I put my total trust in Jesus. More than gratitude for comfort and a good state of mind, I was so grateful that the Lord allowed me to be a witness that day to the whole surgical team who were going to take care of me.

When the anesthesiologist finally entered the room to put me to sleep, the nurse said to him, "Dell sings and we were just listening to some of his music." The last thing I remember before drifting off was the anesthesiologist asking, "What kind of music does he sing?" To that they all chimed in—"gospel music."

Today I went back to the hospital and gave the nurse and doctor each one of our CDs. My prayer is that they claim Jesus as their Savior if they don't already.

This entire experience has reminded me that we all can be witnesses wherever we go. I was also reminded once again that even when we find ourselves in unpleasant circumstances and places in life, God can still give us joy for the journey.

During the month of February, we take time to tell that someone special we love them. Let's not forget to tell the Lord that we love Him and keep Him first place in our lives.

Friends – God always can give *Joy for the Journey.*

· STILL WAITING ·

One time I had to call the service manager of a large repair shop. I was so happy a person answered the telephone instead of a machine. She informed me the man I needed to talk with was away from his desk. I was so close, but so far away.

She asked if I'd like to leave a name and number so I gave her my cell phone number and told her my name was Dell. The woman told me he would call me right back. I believed her.

Four hours later they still had not called me back. Some of you are probably not surprised, but I am a very optimistic person and really thought he'd call back in ten or fifteen minutes.

I finally decided I'd waited long enough and started the process over again. A machine answered. I pushed a few buttons and a live person finally came on the line which was certainly a welcome sound. I explained that I was trying to reach Ed, the service manager. She told me Ed had gone to lunch, but she thought Josh could help me. Before I could say anything, I was on hold listening to music.

Every once in a while, the music would stop and I would think somebody was coming on the line. Instead, I'd hear a recording telling me that my call was important to them, to stay on the line, and somebody would help me.

I couldn't help but think that if my call were all that important to them, I wouldn't still be on hold after ten minutes.

Finally, a voice came on the line and I heard a woman say, "Hello, Mr. Rich." I said, "No, this is Dell and I'm holding for Ed, but I think they are connecting me to Josh." She said she was so sorry and to please hold and the music started again!

Someone finally came back on the line and said she couldn't find Josh, but Ed was back in his office and she would connect me to him. I said, "That's great because that's who I wanted in the first place."

When Ed finally answered the phone, I wasn't sure if I wanted to reach through the line and choke him or hug him, but I got right to business and told him I needed an appointment.

Ed said he needed a little information and then asked my telephone number and name. I spelled H-Y-S-S-O-N-G and said my first name was Dell. He then said, "Oh, I got your message this morning, but put it on the bottom of my call pile because I thought you were calling from Dell computers and wondered what they were trying to sell me now."

We both laughed and then he gave me the appointment I needed. I may not own a computer company and I had to wait half the day to get my appointment, but I still can enjoy life and have *Joy for the Journey.*

· Round Up ·

While traveling thousands of miles on highways each year, we frequently see accidents and road closures. Many times we have stopped for hours on the highway waiting for wreckage to be cleared. Recently we were detoured for miles through the countryside because clearing two eighteen-wheelers and a car that were all overturned was going to take so much time.

When this happens, I reach for the CB radio. The only time we turn on the radio is during accidents because of the terrible language we hear. I use it to find out where the accident is and what lane is best to use to get through the problem.

The first week of January, we were traveling down I-75 to Florida when we noticed all of the traffic in front of us was stopped. I turned on the CB just in time to hear a trucker announce where the accident had occurred and that the cause was a cattle truck that had gone off the road and overturned. The next thing we heard was that both the northbound and southbound lanes were closed because the cattle had gotten loose and were running everywhere.

Can you imagine all those cattle running around? They were free and enjoying their freedom!

We were on a time schedule, but all we could do was wait, albeit not too patiently. We turned off the engine and sat in what we later learned was a ten-mile back-up. Once in a while we would turn the CB back on to see if we could hear what was going on.

The language was disgusting and the news was not encouraging.

The truckers were frustrated and were losing time, money, and patience. After one profane outburst, we heard another trucker's voice say, "Please don't talk like that, you are using my Savior's name."

I listened a little longer as silence reigned on the air. Finally, the Christian trucker came back on again and asked the others to stay quiet because he was going to pray.

He prayed for the truckers who were involved in the accident as well as for patience and safety for all the others stalled in the "parking lot" of I-75.

As I turned off the CB, I thought how one man made a difference and shone God's light in a very dark and difficult situation.

The traffic finally began to move and as we started inching forward, we could see a dozen eighteen-wheelers were lined up to make a fence of trucks to prevent the cattle from coming back on the highway and causing more accidents.

I have great joy knowing that I serve a risen Savior. My heart was joy-filled knowing that a trucker was willing to take a bold stand for Christ and pray over the CB. His courageous action surely made an impact on the other drivers.

Let me encourage you to be a light in this sinful world, to make a difference for the Kingdom, and to have *Joy for the Journey.*

· Eek! Snake! ·

I'll never forget the time after a concert, while I was packing the product table, Richard and Susan were rolling cords and packing the sound system on the platform. My daughter-in-law and two grandchildren were on their way there when all of a sudden my wife screamed for me to come quickly. After almost forty years of marriage, I can tell when she needs me immediately! I hurried into the auditorium. My wife exclaimed, "There's a big snake up here!" My grandson, then thirteen-months-old, had been crawling up the stairs when my daughter-in-law saw a snake sticking its head out from under the carpet less than a foot from where he was, and not far from where we had been standing to sing our concert. Remarkably, none of my family was standing on the chairs or the piano! At that moment, I couldn't have agreed more with the words of the late Wendy Bagwell when he asked, "Where do you want another door?"

I quickly ran to the office and they sent three young men to catch and remove the snake. The young men came into the auditorium and one of them stepped on the snake just behind its head. Another of them reached down and picked it up. When he pulled the snake out from under the carpet, we could see the length was about three feet. They took the snake outside where they were going to release it. Now I've always heard that there are some good snakes, but let me go on record as saying my family has never seen one. We are all afraid of snakes!

As we continued to pack our equipment and carry it out, we all carefully watched where we stepped, reached, and placed things.

My daughter-in-law took both grandchildren out to the coach. The snake and the experience were all that my granddaughter, Makayla, talked about for hours. You would have thought there were hundreds of snakes instead of just one.

We were invited back to sing next year and I can assure you we will be on the lookout for our sinuous friend. We might even do the Mexican hat dance across the platform to make sure there are no snakes under the carpet.

I can't help but think that Satan and sin often rear their ugly heads just like that snake. We should run and flee just like we did from that snake, but sometimes we think that we can dabble in sin and God will still bless us. That could not be farther from the truth. We need to run from sin as we did the snake and follow God's will for our lives.

Snakes and other reptiles may not be our favorite creatures, but every time I think about my wife's scream, the removal of the snake, and God keeping my grandson safe, I have so much to make me smile and praise the Lord.

May God bless you and I trust you have *Joy for the Journey.*

· MISSION: MAINE ·

Some people are quick to say, "It can't be done." Others tell us "we've never done it that way" or "methods are changing and we need to keep up with the times."

In April, 2013, our family was asked to sing at an evangelistic crusade with a prominent evangelist. Following the meeting we talked about teaming up for one month and covering the state of Maine with one-night rallies to see people saved and energize the believers.

Perhaps you ask yourself, *Why Maine?* There are two major reasons for the choice of this large state.

First: A recent report related the State of Maine has fewer residents claiming a religious affiliation than any other state in the union. Maine is the only state in the country where fewer than thirty percent of the population belong to a religious denomination or independent Christian church according to a census conducted by the Association of the Statisticians of American Religious Bodies.

The second reason we chose Maine is that both the evangelist and our family have homes in the state.

Sixteen high school auditoriums and churches were chosen throughout the state as sites and two years were spent in prayer and planning.

Believe me or not, some people and pastors told us we'd not be successful. We were even told that evangelism was for the '60s and

'70s, but not for today.

I kept thinking about the Israelites who got to the Promised Land and refused to go in because of the negative report by ten of the twelve spies. They were on the brink of blessing and saw the obstacles instead of the opportunities.

We kept our eyes on the Lord and never doubted what God could and would do through these meetings.

Space won't permit me to tell you all that happened at Mission: Maine in April, but one Sunday night in Newport, we arrived at the high school and began setting up in the gymnasium that was rented for us. Chairs were set up on the floor of the gym and when the doors opened, people kept coming and coming. The chairs were filled and then the bleachers on each side.

We sang a mini-concert and the evangelist preached. When the invitation to accept Christ was given, the response was incredible. Then Christians were challenged—the response was amazing! While we were leading "Just As I Am," people began flooding to the front of the auditorium. My voice cracked as I wiped a tear from my eye in joyous celebration.

Five days later we held a rally at an elegant banquet facility. The only requirement for a free meal was that Christians had to bring an unsaved person. Sixty-three people accepted Christ that night.

Evangelism and soul-winning are not for the past. They're for now and are exactly what God commands us to do in His Word. Our goal is to keep singing, speaking, and sharing the gospel. When we obey His Word, we will have *Joy for the Journey.*

· MY BAD! ·

Mistakes are an opportunity to learn and do better. At least that's the principle that my son, Richard, was trying to follow before things went terribly wrong.

With all the equipment we have to unload, set up, take down, and load back up at each concert, you might think we would forget things once and a while and leave them behind. Believe me or not, we have not forgotten that many things in the years we have been traveling even though we sing about two hundred fifty concerts each year.

However, one night after we finished singing, Richard took off his suit jacket and threw it over a chair. Then he rolled up some cords, carried out equipment, and you've already guessed that we were at least a hundred miles down the road before he remembered the jacket was still on the back of the chair in the auditorium. So he made some calls and the pastor said he would get the jacket and mail it to us.

No matter how old our kids get, we somehow think it's our job to lecture them about their mistakes. Before you think I'm a bad dad, let me tell you that I've always tried to find the positive and encourage him. Perhaps that's why he has stood by my side singing gospel music for almost twenty years. But that night I told him that he was irresponsible to leave his jacket behind and he needed to pick up after himself and be more careful.

I guess he learned his lesson because the very next Sunday morning he took his suit jacket off and placed it over the pew. After packing up, he went back in the sanctuary and diligently picked up the suit jacket on the pew and brought it with him.

We were an hour down the road when the cell phone rang and the pastor said, "Did someone take my suit jacket?" He went on to tell us the suit was brand new, he'd purchased it to wear for a funeral the next day, and his paycheck from the church was in the inside top pocket.

Richard said, "No, I just got my jacket." Then my wife piped up and said, "No, I got your jacket." By mistake, Richard had picked up the pastor's new suit jacket and brought it with him.

We've all heard the expression, "It's either feast or famine." We were either short a jacket or had one too many.

We've laughed about this many times. Believe me when I tell you we haven't left anything behind nor have we picked up extra things since those two events. I guess we have learned from our mistakes.

Learning from our mistakes and not repeating them are important lessons. Instead of being down on ourselves, we also need to remember that God loves and forgives us even when we fall short.

If we live by these Biblical principles, we will have better tomorrows and have Joy for the Journey.

• Jumping to Judgment •

B eing on the road as much as we are, we appreciate having good neighbors. They will often pick up our mail and packages, and even watch for intruders while we are away.

Richard has a neighbor two doors down the street who watches his house and everyone else's in the neighborhood.

Recently the neighbor became suspicious when he saw a disheveled old man in the backyard of the house between his house and Richard's. After noticing the parent's car was gone, he realized the old man was chasing the young child who lived there. When the child ran into the house, the old man followed right after him.

The neighbor who was watching got very nervous and ran out to his car. He drove quickly to a road directly behind the houses and watched intently as the commotion continued in the house.

He could see the old man chasing the child through the house and he heard screaming and shouting. Drawers were being rummaged through and all of a sudden he could see the cellar door open and the old man chased the child down the stairs and out of sight.

The neighbor's heart was pounding as he dialed 9-1-1. His voice was shaking as he reported what he was watching.

Then he decided to drive back to his own house and wait for the police to arrive. Not long after he'd called, several police cars arrived and surrounded the house. The police approached with caution, but everything changed when they saw blood splattered all over the deck.

Now guns were drawn and more backup was summoned. As the police entered, announced their presence, and demanded the old man to give himself up, voices could still be heard in the basement.

All of the other neighbors were told to stay inside their homes while watching the drama unfold.

We found out that the old man was the child's grandfather and they were cutting the dog's nails. They cut the nail too short and it began to bleed. The dog got away and the child and grandfather were chasing the dog, yelling for him to stop, and trying to grab a rag or bandage out of the drawers to wrap around the paw.

The neighbor didn't want anyone to know he had called 9-1-1; however everyone knew Jack had made the call.

There is a lesson here for us all. All of the evidence that day pointed to something quite different from what was actually happening. The Bible warns us to control our tongues. Yet, sometimes we gossip, talk about people, and assume things that are not true. Gossip can be so hurtful and ruin a reputation. We need to make sure we have all the facts before we jump to conclusions.

On the positive side, we should all watch out for our neighbors because the Bible tells us to be kind and help one another.

Until next month; enjoy your summer, laugh a little, and have *Joy for the Journey.*

• Rewards Postponed •

When I mow the lawn, I find looking behind me satisfying and rewarding because I can see the results immediately. I wish I felt the same way when I sing a song, preach a sermon, or write an article, but often it is a long time before I see results. Some of us will not see the results or the change in someone's life this side of heaven.

If you are a pastor, Sunday school teacher, youth worker, singer, or writer you know exactly what I am saying. Sometimes your job probably seems thankless and you wonder, like I have, "Is it worth it?" The hymn writer wrote, "it will be worth it all when we see Jesus," but it's great to see results and know that you are making a difference right now.

Recently we traveled a lot of miles to reach our concert date. We were exhausted as we set up and got ready for the concert. We were in that city for the first time and didn't know anyone there.

I was surprised when a man came into the auditorium and started to tell me his story. He shared how his grown son had gotten into drugs. His voice grew even more serious when he told about the day when the police came to his house and arrested his son. He explained how they had handcuffed his son and led him away.

After this event, the man fell into a deep depression and said he was at the lowest point in his life. He felt the need to get away from home, so he left his family and drove off to a remote cabin that they owned.

He was lying on his bed in the cabin, crying and broken-hearted when all of a sudden he reached over to his nightstand and picked up a magazine that a friend had given him. He flipped through the pages and started to read *Joy for the Journey* in the *Christian Voice Magazine*.

He told me how that particular article ministered to him and changed his life. His life went from the depths of despair to victory and rejoicing as he turned his eyes to the Lord.

The man stared at me and said he couldn't believe the Lord was allowing him to meet the person who had written the article.

Today he is at home with his family and helping his son who is on probation. He has gotten deeply involved with his church and has taken his eyes off himself and onto the Savior.

Next time we question the worth of preaching that sermon, teaching that class, or singing that song, remember the story of this man who discovered joy for the journey because I took the time to write an article. That article encouraged a man that I had never met and may never see this side of heaven again. The change in his life and the story he told has given us both *Joy for the Journey.*

· Happiness is a Choice ·

I've always been told there is a difference between happiness and joy. Sometimes we confuse the two, which often leads us to feel disappointed.

Happiness comes as a result of things that happen to and around us. Outside events can make us happy or sad depending on our attitude about them. Happiness is a choice.

For example, I remember when my five-year-old granddaughter came to me during a sound check and asked, "Grandpa, can I sing with you tonight?"

I'd waited for five years to hear those words. So that night we got out another microphone, she came up for one song and sang her little heart out.

That is the kind of event that brings happiness. In contrast, she is the same granddaughter who was born with tumors in her heart and brain. When she was born, I had a heavy heart and was sad. But God miraculously healed her. Happiness was mine.

I write all of that to say we should never confuse happiness with joy.

My articles are titled *Joy for the Journey*. Joy is something that happens on the inside. Joy, peace, and contentment come from knowing God. When Makayla was born and we learned of the difficulties facing her, I was very sad; however, I still had joy about the gift God had given us in our baby granddaughter.

Even when outside circumstances don't make me happy, I can still have the joy of the Lord if I know Jesus Christ personally.

A couple of years ago I wrote about a paraplegic who seemed to have lost everything twenty-seven years ago when he had a sledding accident.

The first snow storm of the year was an occasion for happiness. He'd jumped on a sled and begun to slide rapidly down the hill. On the way down, he'd crashed into a tree and, we would think, lost everything.

He lost the use of his legs and arms, lost his job, his fiancée, and all his independence. But my friends, he has never lost his joy!

We had not seen him for a couple of years when his dad wheeled him into one of our concerts recently.

He has been an inspiration to me over the years, so I quickly made my way over to where he was sitting. The wheelchair and his body are stark reminders of that horrible accident years ago. His attitude, however, is always uplifting. He's quick to tell you that he may look like he lost everything, but he never lost Jesus.

We sang the familiar song, "Through It All," that night, and I couldn't help but watch our friend as he sang along with us. "Through it all, through it all, I've learned to trust in Jesus, I've learned to trust in God."

Outwardly our friend has nothing to make him happy. But on the inside…! He has the peace, joy, and contentment that God gives.

When we know and trust in God, we all can have *Joy for the Journey*.

· Thanks for the Ministry ·

November has traditionally been a month of Thanksgiving—the time to give thanks to Almighty God for all of His blessings. We are especially grateful this year to sing for the Lord.

I could go on and on to tell you about God's blessings upon my ministry, family, and life. Today I'm writing to tell you about a special blessing that gave me so much joy.

We have the privilege to sing at several fairs each year. Recently we returned to a fair that we had sung at last year.

While we were setting up, a man came up to the stage and said he had heard us last year. He told us that his wife didn't even think she wanted to sit down and listen to the music, but when it was over, she bought sixty dollars' worth of our CDs. I joked with him and told him I liked his wife already.

He continued to tell me that he drove a transportation van that took elderly people and children to appointments. Drivers are not allowed to talk about religion or politics, but they can listen to anything they'd like on the radio. So after hearing our concert last year, he started playing our CDs in the van.

One elderly lady became a regular rider with him. After several trips, she began to ask him questions. She told him that she had gone to church all of her life but had never heard words with such meaning in her church as those in the songs.

The driver and his wife had the wonderful privilege of leading the woman to Christ—three months later the woman died. This couple said they were so glad to know that when she closed her eyes here on this earth, she opened them again to find herself in the presence of Jesus.

The man said, "I had to come see you today because one day when you get to heaven, a lady is going to thank you for your music that brought her to Christ. You never met her and didn't know her, but she knew you and was so thankful for your ministry."

I stood there totally blown away by his story. As he walked away, I thanked the Lord for the encouraging words. A woman got saved at the end of her life because this couple had come to a fair, attended our concert, bought some music, boldly played our CD in their van, and willingly answered the questions of a woman searching for life's answers.

The Bible says that some plant, some water, and some bring the increase. I'm just glad that God gave us the chance to be a part of the process that resulted in a woman getting saved.

There was no doubt that the couple talking to me had the joy of the Lord in their lives. I was blessed by their story and I am thankful this Thanksgiving for the way God gives *Joy for the Journey.*

· NEED VS. GREED ·

The other day, I was visiting friends who had just remodeled their home. Their little five-year-old boy seemed perplexed—I could tell he was deep in thought. I asked what he was thinking about and he told me the chimney had been removed. He wondered how Santa was going to get into his house with no chimney to slide down.

I answered by telling him Santa knew where he lived and wouldn't miss the opportunity to bring him some gifts. That seemed to satisfy the little boy. I finished our talk by encouraging him to leave Santa some milk and cookies.

My five-year-old granddaughter had just lost two front teeth. So that year her song was definitely, "All I Want for Christmas is My Two Front Teeth. "

To see Christmas through the eyes of a child is so much fun. I love Christmas and we enjoy spending time together as a family.

In sharp contrast, a lady just talked to me about her preparations for Christmas. She told me she had eleven grandchildren and she had to spend a great deal of money to buy them all the gifts. She said she had many gifts already purchased and others on lay-a-way. To her, Christmas is a time to buy and spend. In fact, she was concerned she wouldn't have enough money and her credit card would be maxed-out. How sad people feel that they have to go into debt to celebrate Christmas.

As I walked away from her, I couldn't help but think to myself, *how could we have come so far from that starry night in Bethlehem?*

There is only one gift that really matters at Christmas. That gift was given to each one of us when God gave us His only begotten Son, Jesus Christ, who was born to be the Savior of the world.

For unto you is born this day in the city of David, a Saviour, which is Christ the Lord. (Luke 2:11 KJV)

Christmas isn't about Santa, it's about a Savior. Christmas isn't about how much we can spend on gifts, it's about the greatest gift ever given.

As much fun as we have seeing Christmas through the eyes of a child, it's far greater to see Christmas through the eyes of a "Child of God."

Our Christmas will be simple this year. We will sing on Christmas Eve about an hour from home. Following our Christmas Eve concert, we will go home to spend time with the family. My Mom (eighty-eight years old), Dad (eighty-nine years old), our son, daughter-in-law, two grandchildren, and my wife and I will read Luke 2, exchange gifts we can afford, and enjoy a big Christmas dinner.

I can't encourage you enough to keep "Christ in Christmas" and center your celebrations on Him. Don't be trapped by the trappings. When your Christmas is about Christ, you will be able to sing "Joy to the World" and ultimately have *Joy for the Journey.*

Merry Christmas from the Hyssongs!

• Funny but Foolish •

I was always told in school by my teachers, "there are no foolish questions." I've often wondered about the truth of that statement. Sometimes classmates would ask questions that I thought were foolish. Others would raise their hands and ask questions while we waited to be dismissed for lunch or recess. Situations that have happened recently cause me to question its veracity.

We were invited to sing at a church and arrived early to set up. Everything was ready for the concert and people started to arrive. My son and I were standing behind our product table and greeting people as they came in. One young man shook our hands and asked two questions.

First he said, "Are you guys singing here tonight?" Then he looked at our CDs, picked one up, looked at our pictures, and said, "Are you singing on these?"

I didn't know whether I should say, *No, they used our pictures, but someone else is singing* or if I should say, *we just hum on those CDs.* But I was good and just said, "Yes, our family sings and we are glad to be here tonight."

Perhaps you are saying that's not so bad. Well, let me tell you a story that beats the previous one. A foolish question wasn't what got my attention, but rather a foolish action. We arrived for another concert and discovered the auditorium was on the second floor. That would have been okay except the elevators had a huge sign on the doors at eye level saying, DO NOT USE—OUT OF

ORDER.

We dragged all of our equipment up the stairs and set up. Everyone climbed the stairs without any complaints, the place was full, and we had a great concert.

Following the concert, we were selling CDs and people were going down the stairs except for one lady. She went to the elevators and pushed the button. The door opened and she entered without hesitation. Then the doors closed behind her and she thought she was on her way down. At least that's what I thought as I continued to talk with people and sell our product.

I changed my mind when fire trucks, police cars, and an ambulance arrived with sirens blaring.

After quite a while, they got her out. Can you imagine how embarrassed she must have been?

Don't you wonder what she was thinking? Perhaps she thought, *that sign doesn't apply to me*, or *I'm glad the people are all taking the stairs so I can get right into the elevator.* Apparently my teachers were wrong. You can do things and ask questions that are foolish. Friends, I couldn't make this up. Sometimes I have to just chuckle and shake my head.

Seriously, I love the Lord and love people. This year I want to put the Lord above everything else and do things and say things that bring honor to God. I pray you will have a Happy New Year and *Joy for the Journey.*

• THE TEMPERATURE'S RISING •

Winter weather with all of the ice and snow can cause all kinds of travel and driving problems for singers and concert attendees. Pastors and promoters also have difficulty deciding whether to cancel or continue with a scheduled concert.

In December, we were faced with the difficult decision of going or canceling twice. We did cancel one weekend due to a strong winter storm through the Northeast.

On the other weekend in North Carolina, according to the forecast, we were likely to receive freezing rain and possibly snow. We made the decision to drive to the concert and see how many people would attend. If we needed to stay overnight, we would do so because we always put safety at the top of our list. However, we really needed to get back to Tennessee for a Christmas event where we were scheduled to sing the next night. If we drove through the night, we would have to drive through the Gorge on Route 40. That twenty-mile stretch of road is not my favorite to drive. Freezing rain would only make things more dangerous.

That night the church was filled with people and beautifully decorated for Christmas. There was a wonderful spirit in the air as we sang our Christmas concert ending with "O Holy Night."

The pastor stood to pray and dismiss the audience. Before he prayed he looked out at the crowd and said, "This group has to drive through the Gorge tonight and I want you all to agree that you will pray for them for the next hour." As the preacher prayed, he asked God to give us safety and then boldly asked God to keep the temperature above freezing and even go up to fifty degrees.

We packed our equipment, talked for a while, and got into our vehicle to begin our trip. We had decided to start out and stop before the Gorge if the weather got too bad.

There is a temperature gauge on the dashboard of our vehicle that we kept a close eye on as we began our journey. I looked down at the dash and saw thirty-seven degrees. If the temperature dropped further, we would get into trouble very quickly. However, as we started through the Gorge, the temperature started to rise. All three of us watched the temperature go up one degree at a time until it reached fifty-one degrees! I can't describe the excitement and feelings that we had as the temperature climbed. We were seeing God at work.

My son picked up the cell phone and called the pastor to thank him for praying and asking his people to pray for our safety. God had heard their prayers and answered in a miraculous way.

We got to the bottom of the Gorge and as we entered Tennessee, the temperature dropped ten degrees within a minute.

Friends, God still answers prayer. Believe me when I say, "He is still in the miracle-working business and gives *Joy for the Journey*.

• God's in Control •

Gospel singers are always looking for songs that will reach the hearts of their audiences. If a song speaks to me, I hope the song will touch others as well.

Today, Christians are concerned about their health care, are worried about the economy, and are watching the Middle East with great interest. So often people worry and fret and forget the Biblical truth that God is still on the throne and in control.

When we came across a song entitled, "God's in Control," we knew the message was good, but we had no idea what an impact the music would make on people's lives when they heard it at our concerts and on the radio.

I can't express the joy that our family receives when we hear from our friends how a song or our ministry has made a difference in their lives. I hope you're encouraged too as you read the following e-mail and Facebook messages that we have recently received.

"Hello from Ohio: I wanted to share something with your family. I would appreciate if you would remember me in prayer. I have done something to my right hip and am kind of laid up. We are in the middle of farming. I had to have an MRI this morning. MRIs and I do not get along very well, as I am claustrophobic. While in the testing, I requested *Enlighten* as the music for them to play (the hospital has Sirius radio). While I was strapped down, my hip locked up and I started sweating. I remembered my precious sister before she went to heaven, always said "The Lord's Prayer" and that helped her through tests. Well, I started repeating "The Lord's Prayer" and crying 'cause I miss her so much. The technician wanted to stop the MRI, but I said no, we have to finish this 'cause I cannot start all over again. While lying there praying and crying, your song came on ("God's in Control") and He took over. The pain subsided, I quit sweating, and my tears became tears of gratitude—thanking Him for watching over me. Praise the Lord for the many blessings that He has bestowed upon me. One of the blessings is having met your wonderful family."

A young man from North Carolina wrote: "I'm driving to work and it's five forty-five a.m. I figured you and your family should hear this. Recently I've been called to preach. Your song, "God's in Control," came on the radio and I wept because I've been so nervous about preaching and didn't want to be a failure. But now I'm reminded He has everything under control for today and the days ahead of me."

To this man and woman and so many others who have written to us—thank you! As the hymn writer wrote, "There is Joy in Serving Jesus."

I trust that as we are reminded that God is in control, all of us will stop fretting and have *Joy for the Journey.*

• BAHAMAS MELODY •

During the first week of February, our family was to perform on a gospel music cruise to the Bahamas.

A few days before the cruise, the Freeport Bahamas Pastor's Association heard that gospel groups were scheduled to stop at the Port of Freeport. They quickly emailed the promoters to invite three groups to perform on the island.

On February 3rd, the Roarks, Eternal Vision, and our family, The Hyssongs, were to be escorted to the Port Lucaya Marketplace stage at Count Basie Square. We were excited about the invitation and opportunity and started getting ready to leave the ship. Everyone was allowed off except my son and me. They would not allow us to take our trumpet and trombone off the ship.

Special permission and paperwork filled out by Bahamas customs agents would be required for us to be allowed to take the instruments off with us. They sent us back upstairs while the others waited outside for the van to arrive that would take them to the stage in the middle of the shopping district.

At first we were told the procedure would take ten minutes, but later we learned two hours was more probable with the possibility that the request would be denied. My son and I sat on the ship at the purser's desk waiting for word, wondering if the group had left us behind and if we'd ever get permission to leave with the instruments.

The time seemed to be flying and the concert was to start at twelve noon. We wondered if we would be able to catch up with the group if we got permission or how much a taxi would cost if we were left behind.

Finally, all of the paperwork was completed and we were set to go. When we got off the ship, to our surprise the group was all waiting for us. Even though the ship told us they were working on the paperwork, the local pastor was the one who had gone to the head customs agent to get our instruments released.

We all jumped into a minibus and had the ride of our lives. Riding in a van driving on the left side of the road at those speeds is an experience we will never forget.

We got to the stage on time but still waited. Apparently, island time meant everything starts twenty minutes late. Those of you who travel know what I mean.

Many locals, as well as many passengers from other cruise ships, enjoyed the hour-long concert. The music was also broadcast throughout all the stores and restaurants in the area. The Freeport pastor was thrilled that the gospel of Jesus Christ was sung and spoken openly in such a public arena!

We have all been invited to return for future concerts in Freeport, as well as other surrounding islands.

As our radio song proclaims, "God's in Control." Our three groups had an unforgettable time and we all agree that we had *Joy for the Journey.*

• THE DARKEST HOUR •

Just when you think you've seen everything, something else happens that makes you step back and scratch your head.

We drove into the parking lot of the church where we were scheduled to sing one Sunday night. No one was there, so we called the pastor to let him know we had arrived. The pastor answered the telephone by saying, "I'm glad you are here, this has been the worst day of my life. We need you to lead us in worship."

Not long after that the pastor arrived at the church. He explained how several people had resigned from the church that morning—including his treasurer. Apparently some people had even accused the pastor of stealing some money. One word that came to mind was *awkward,* but the situation got worse.

The pastor came in and sat in the front pew, talking to us while we set up our equipment.

All of a sudden, the side door opened and his wife stepped in with what looked to be several pages of financial records.

The pastor excused himself and told us he had to attend an unexpected emergency meeting. Cars started arriving and more than forty people came to the meeting.

We have no idea what happened, but ten minutes before the concert was to start, the pastor reappeared and sat in the front row weeping. I sat beside him trying to console him, but to no avail. Ten minutes after we were to start, he still sat there. I asked if he was going to start the service and he said he was waiting for the others to come in.

My son told him all the people who had come for the meeting said they wouldn't be coming to the concert. That made him cry even harder.

There were many visitors present for the concert and the time was getting later and later. We were way overdue to begin. I finally said, "Let us just start the concert with no introductions." His wife leaned over and said, "That would be great! Can you pray too?"

As we sang our last song, the pastor got out his keys and put on his jacket. On the last note of our song, he bolted out the side door.

As I already mentioned, the evening was tough and awkward. In fact, I tried to figure out how all this could be tied to Joy for the Journey. But God was working even then. A few days later, I called the pastor to see how he was doing. He thanked us for helping the church and him during one of its darkest hours.

I still scratched my head but knew that God never makes mistakes. If God used us to bring a little bit of joy and healing, then all the awkwardness was worth it. Without a doubt, when we are doing what God wants us to do and we are where He wants us to be, God gives us *Joy for the Journey.*

· ANGELS ALL AROUND US ·

The Bible tells us about angels. I do believe there are angels watching over us. Looking back over my life, I can think about several times when angels were protecting me and taking care of me and my family. On a couple of occasions, I believe I was entertaining or seeing angels unaware.

Once while I was crossing a border into a foreign country, someone in uniform appeared out of nowhere, walked over, and told me to pull into another lane and keep going. Thinking back, I don't know where he came from or where he disappeared to. I wasn't even questioned or searched. Could that have been an angel?

Recently I heard a story worth retelling to you.

A World War II veteran shared with us he was taken as a prisoner in battle. Shortly after being taken captive, the Americans were lined up before a German firing squad. Horror still colored his voice as he related the enemy were shooting one man after another as they came down the line toward him. They arrived at him and put a gun to his head. Scared and shaking, he told he just wanted it to be over.

At that very moment, an officer from the German army came out of the woods, held up his hand and spoke a few words. The squad lowered their weapons and stopped the executions. The officer then walked back into the woods.

Not long after this event occurred, the Allied forces began to attack the prison camp where he had been held captive. During the attack, he was able to free himself and escape unharmed. He was free! Continuing the story, he told of how he walked and walked until he was finally picked up by our troops.

I don't know about you, but I have several thoughts. First, I'm thankful for the countless men and women who have served our country in the past and for all those who still serve today.

Secondly, I wonder if an angel, not a German officer, stepped out of the woods to stop the firing squad. All he did was hold up his hand and speak a few words. We will probably never know this side of heaven, but I certainly am thankful for God's protective hand that day and the angels that watched over him and who watch over me day after day.

Many of us have sung a gospel song by Legacy Five entitled, "God's Been Good." In the second verse, they sing about being through trying times and crying bitter tears. They then go on to sing that God's arms were around them as they faced great fears.

Friends, we've all faced some of those fears. Maybe you've faced financial fears or physical fears or fears for your family, but what a comfort to know the arms of God and his mighty force of angels are watching over us.

When we grasp that great knowledge and truth, we can have *Joy for the Journey.*

• Reunited •

All of us cross paths with people who impact and influence us throughout our lives.

In 1974, I was in college working toward my music degree with a concentration in voice. One day the chairman of the music department told me they were interviewing a new professor. He wondered if I would let her give me a voice lesson while they observed.

Looking back, I know we were both nervous, but she did a great job and became my voice teacher for my two remaining years of college.

Holly Weiss was a wonderful teacher. I wish I could say that I always worked hard and did my best, but like a lot of college students there were times when I was more interested in dating my future wife, Susan, and having a good time.

My voice professor was patient, kind, and did her best to keep me focused. She was not only a good teacher, she was a phenomenal singer. We asked her to sing at our wedding when Susan and I married one week after graduation. She accepted—her solos were an incredible part of our ceremony.

All that happened many years ago. We'd not seen her since our wedding, although we'd heard she was singing opera in New York City and still giving voice lessons.

A couple of weeks ago I received a surprising email from our voice professor. She shared that she had seen our poster and was glad to know we were going to be singing near her. After all those years, she was going to attend our concert and we'd see her again! Finally, we'd be able to thank her for the impact and influence she'd had on our lives when we were in college.

When people began arriving, I wondered if we would recognize her, but when she stepped in wearing her unforgettable smile, we rushed to give her hugs.

Now I had another concern. We were classically trained. Susan played Rachmaninoff and Bach and I sang arias and classical music. How was our professor going to respond to our gospel music? Her smile and enthusiasm that night put our minds at ease right away. Following the concert, her compliments and support were overwhelming. There is no doubt that she has the gift of encouragement.

All these years later we had the chance to say thank you. God had placed her in our lives many years ago to prepare us for the ministry we have today.

Since that reunion, we have regularly emailed and she is going to have a huge part in our ministry for the next couple of years. People may not meet her or see her, but we are excited for her support and help in the background.

I cannot urge each of you enough to find and thank those people who have influenced you in the past. If they have passed away— thank God for them. We thank God for Holly Weiss, who has given us *Joy for the Journey*.

· Timing is Everything ·

A beautiful chorus entitled, "In His Time," tells us that God makes all things beautiful in his time. We know God's timing is perfect and He never makes mistakes. Ecclesiastes Chapter 3 clearly states there is a time for everything under the sun.

We may never understand many of the things that come into our lives this side of heaven, but I have no doubt in my mind that God has a purpose and plan for each of us.

Recently my son, Richard, and I were asked by a radio station to come and help them for a few hours with their Share-a-Thon. We thought we would donate a couple of our CDs to use for give-a-ways during our time on the air. We had a lot of fun as we began our time together with the DJ. He played music, we talked to the listeners, and, of course, also shared the need for the public to support that radio station.

Midway through the morning, we decided to change things up and offer one of our CDs to the fourth listener to call into the station.

The telephone lines lit up and the winner was announced shortly after that. A little bit later, we noticed a woman standing outside the glassed-in studio watching us. During the next song, we opened the door—she said she was the one who had called in and won the free CD. She continued to explain she and her children were listening to the station while driving and were just about to get on the turnpike when they called in and won. So she turned around and drove back the few miles to pick up the recording in person. We all shook hands and were glad to meet her. However, we couldn't talk long because we needed to go back on the air.

About thirty minutes later the station secretary came in and told us that the woman had just called back with an amazing story.

Before turning around to come and get her CD, she and her children had been following a large truck. When she returned to where she had been when she made the call and won, she realized that there had been a horrific accident involving that truck. The woman wanted us to know that if she hadn't won the CD and come to the station to pick it up, she believed that her family would have been involved in the accident.

Oft times we will not know this side of heaven why certain things happen in our lives, but that lady knew exactly why God allowed her to win the CD and led her to turn back. She was praising God and giving Him the glory.

Many things I may not understand, but I know that God loves us. I believe He directs our steps. When we trust in Him and believe His timing is perfect (no matter what comes into our lives), we will have *Joy for the Journey.*

• 'Til the Storm Passes By •

I 've often read the Bible story about the disciples' fear when they were in a boat while a fierce storm raged and the winds blew. Recently we had an experience that reminded me how safe they were and how safe we are in God's hands.

In July, we were on the road, watching the ominous-looking sky. Something told me to pull off the highway, so I pulled into a campground. We seldom use campgrounds, but we had an extra day before our next concert.

My grandchildren were thrilled to see a playground. They played while we set up and settled in for the night. As the sun set, everyone headed back to the motorhome for a bite to eat and to watch some television.

Suddenly we looked out our front window—across the field we could see a dark cloud and heavy rain coming toward us. A herd of cows that had been grazing nearby took off running toward the barn faster than I've ever seen cows run in my life. They obviously sensed something in the air. The sky looked so threatening that our family immediately prayed and asked God to protect us.

Then the storm hit hard. Rain poured down from the sky and very strong winds began to blow and swirl. Immediately the power went off—we all watched out the windows as large trees snapped and fell like twigs. Within two or three minutes, the whole area looked like a war zone. Trees, branches, and benches were scattered everywhere. We must have been caught in a mini-tornado—

the feeling was so surreal.

As quickly as the winds and rain came upon us, the storm was over and gone. People all over the park came out of their trailers and motorhomes to assess the damage. They removed debris from the roadway as well as helped people remove trees from their tents, cars, and destroyed awnings.

Our family walked around the campground surveying the damage as everyone made sure people were not hurt. We realized a whole line of trees had blown down on the road beside us, and that as the wind had turned, the trees were all blown down behind us. Everything had missed us by only a few yards.

The electricity never did come back on that night, but we ran our generator and had air conditioners to keep us cool. The power might not have come back on, but we saw a different power—the awesome power of Almighty God and His mighty hand of protection upon us.

Deuteronomy 6:7 reminded the Israelites to talk to their children about God *when you sit in your house, when you walk by the way, when you lie down, and when you rise up.*

My grandchildren may not have fully realized how God had protected us that evening, but we will tell them many times so they follow and love the Lord with all their hearts. As they follow Him, we will have *Joy for the Journey.*

• TOO MUCH INFORMATION •

How you can communicate with people at the touch of a button is amazing. E-mail has changed the way we correspond. When I hadn't even figured out how cell phones worked, we moved into Skype—where we can see the person we are talking to. I don't want you to think that I'm ignorant when I say I don't understand the cell phone, but how does my voice bounce off some tower and reach around the world with clarity?

Today social media has become a huge activity—everybody is using Facebook, Twitter, and LinkedIn. You can use smartphones, tablets, and computers to send messages, videos, and pictures.

We use social media to let people know our schedule and when we are going to be in their areas. Occasionally we also place pictures on our Facebook page so people can see the family and the places we are traveling.

A pet peeve of mine is when people think I want to read what they ate for breakfast or how they spent every minute of the day.

A while ago, we read someone's Facebook page where they blasted their ex-husband and shared their new-found friend and love-of-their-life. Posting that was certainly not Christian or appropriate to put out for all the world to read. The ongoing post disgusted us and in no way gave us joy for our journey. The content of the messages and the poor grammar were just deplorable.

Recently we experienced why we need to be careful in this new world of communication. One of our drivers was on a ten-day road trip with us. His wedding anniversary happened to fall in the middle of the trip. He wrote a Facebook message to his wife and told her that he missed her, loved her, and wished she was with him. After putting much thought into the anniversary message, he posted it on her timeline.

Not long after the posting, a friend called his cell phone and said, "Why did you post this love note to my wife?" The conversation was like an old *I Love Lucy* TV show where everything was based on misunderstandings. We had a red-faced driver when he realized he had sent the message intended for his wife to the wrong person. The friend was understanding and quickly erased the message. By this time, everyone in our coach—caring, compassionate people—were howling with laughter at all the confusion. The friend and his wife understood the situation was all a mistake.

Social media is a great tool to help us keep in touch with all of our friends, but we need to be careful. Our messages can be read by the world. The Bible tells us to watch our speech. *Put away from you a deceitful mouth and put devious speech far from you.* (Proverbs 4:24, NASB)

God has blessed us with many things that we can use for His glory. We need to ensure we use them properly and so have *Joy for the Journey.*

· One Day at a Time ·

R ecently we had a very long and difficult day. Our trials began when we came upon a big accident. There were police cars, fire engines, and two ambulances on the scene. Debris covered the roadway where two cars had hit head-on. We see lots of accidents on our travels, but this one was very bad.

The blocked road slowed us up, which is always difficult. Even though we were on a time schedule, we were very concerned for the passengers who were removed from the demolished cars and placed in the ambulances.

We always pause and pray for the victims. We are reminded in such instances of the safety God has given to us as we travel thousands of miles each year.

When we finally got going after the accident cleared, we had sinking feelings in the pits of our stomachs. We drove a little slower and were a little more cautious for the rest of the day.

The day started with the car accident and ended with Facebook news about a drug store in our hometown that was under lockdown because a lone gunman was holding an employee hostage.

Our town is small and we know most of the employees, as well as many of the law enforcement officers who were at the scene. As the drama unfolded, we kept following the situation on Facebook and on news feeds from different reporters on the Internet. The whole drama lasted more than six hours before the final hostage was released and the gunman took his own life.

I'm grateful that every day isn't as tough as that one. However, even the hard days can bring better endings.

Recently we were setting up when a young couple came through the door and told us, "We saw you last year. We almost didn't come last year because we had just lost our child, but we did. You sang a song that touched and changed our hearts and lives. We bought that song and listened to you sing every morning just to get us through the day."

They asked if we would sing the song during our concert that night. We honored their request, but there was no way I could look at them as we sang because they were weeping openly.

I can't help but think of the contrast between this couple who had lost a child and the lone gunman.

For the gunman who took his own life, everything seemed hopeless. He went into the drug store that night for drugs that he thought would dull his pain and give him happiness and joy somehow, but offered him nothing.

For the couple who had lost their son—they were both hurting but turned to Christ and a gospel song that gave them real encouragement, hope, and joy.

Sometimes on the road I get weary, but I never get tired of sharing the gospel in song and in the message of Jesus Christ who gives us hope and *Joy for the Journey.*

· More Blessed to Give ·

I t's beginning to look a lot like Christmas, everywhere I go." The lights, decorations, and music are all an indication that Christmas is just around the corner. Most people seem to be a little happier and more cheerful this time of the year—I know I am—I love Christmas!

I say most because all of us occasionally run across an old Scrooge—someone who has missed the whole idea of the season.

We stopped one day at a mall to do a little shopping. My wife, Susan, was shocked by the pushing and shoving. The shopping frenzy got so bad that when she picked up a man's sweater to check out the size, a lady beside her literally ripped the sweater away because she wanted it.

I'll never know if I would have liked the sweater because the other lady took it. I know the Bible reads, *Vengeance is Mine, I will repay, says the Lord.* (Romans 12:19) But down deep I hope she gets a piece of coal in her stocking this Christmas.

What a sharp contrast to an older lady who sends ten dollars each month to our ministry and writes, "I wish it could be more." She can hardly afford to buy food for the table and the medicines she needs, but she gives a sacrificial gift. She shows love and gentle kindness while demonstrating the virtue of selfless giving.

Recently we sang at a ticketed event. A young couple, whom we see about once a year, came to our product table. They have six young children and with tears in their eyes, they told us that today was their anniversary. They didn't know how their children came up with the money or when they had called for the tickets, but their children gave them tickets to our concert. The children had scraped all their money together and given their parents an anniversary gift that they will always remember.

At a young age, those children have put Acts 20:35 into practice, *And remember the words of the Lord Jesus, that He said, "It is more blessed to give than to receive."*

The older lady I mentioned before has learned the same principle. Isn't that what Christmas should be? We give gifts because God gave us the greatest gift of all. He gave His Son to be born in a manger over two thousand years ago. That lowly cradle led to a cross and our salvation, and friends—that is Love.

The lady in the mall took the sweater that my wife wanted to give to me for Christmas, but no one can steal my joy. No one can take away my Savior, given by God to me on that first Christmas morning.

I wish you a very Merry Christmas and joyous New Year. May we remember that it is more blessed to give to others during Christmas and throughout the year than to receive. As we apply this principle, we will have *Joy for the Journey*.